CYBER
Savvy

CYBER Savvy

EMBRACING DIGITAL SAFETY AND CIVILITY

NANCY WILLARD

CORWIN
A SAGE Company

CORWIN
A SAGE Company

FOR INFORMATION:

Corwin
A SAGE Company
2455 Teller Road
Thousand Oaks, California 91320
(800) 233-9936
Fax: (800) 417-2466
www.corwin.com

SAGE Ltd.
1 Oliver's Yard
55 City Road
London EC1Y 1SP
United Kingdom

SAGE India Pvt. Ltd.
B 1/I 1 Mohan Cooperative Industrial Area
Mathura Road, New Delhi 110 044
India

SAGE Asia-Pacific Pte. Ltd.
33 Pekin Street #02–01
Far East Square
Singapore 048763

Acquisitions Editor: Arnis Burvikovs
Associate Editor: Desirée Bartlett
Editorial Assistant: Kimberly Greenberg
Production Editor: Amy Schroller
Copy Editor: Matthew Sullivan
Typesetter: Hurix Systems Pvt. Ltd.
Proofreader: Ellen Howard
Indexer: Sheila Bodell
Cover Designer: Scott Van Atta
Permissions Editor: Karen Ehrmann

Printed in the United States of America.

Library of Congress Cataloging-in-Publication Data

Willard, Nancy E.
Cyber savvy: embracing digital safety and civility/ Nancy Willard.

p. cm.
Includes bibliographical references and index.

ISBN 978-1-4129-9621-1 (pbk.)

1. Internet and children. 2. Internet and teenagers. 3. Internet—Safety measures. 4. Parenting. I. Title.

HQ784.I58W56 2012

004.67'8 0835—dc23

2011034050

This book is printed on acid-free paper.

11 12 13 14 15   10 9 8 7 6 5 4 3 2 1

Contents

A Cyber Savvy website has been set up to support this book at http://embracingdigitalyouth.org. This site provides access to surveys that can be used to support the instructional and evaluation activities suggested in this book, as well as stories and news articles that can be used to stimulate student discussions and a teacher's forum.

Preface

Cyber Savvy: Embracing Digital Safety and Civility provides guidance to educators, mental health professionals, and law enforcement officers on how to effectively implement instructional activities to address these issues of safety and civility with today's digital youth.

The Cyber Savvy instructional approach is grounded in the understanding that the vast majority of young people want to make good choices, do not want to be harmed, and do not want to see their friends or others harmed. This instructional approach focuses on positive social norms, effective practices, and the positive engagement of witnesses. Use of local data, gathered through online surveys of students, will provide insight to guide instruction and positive messaging, as well as provide the ability to engage in ongoing evaluation to ensure effectiveness.

Effective education can help young people be more mindful of the possible consequences of their actions, increase their problem-solving skills, provide insight into effective protective actions and responses, and encourage them to engage in responsible behavior that protects the rights of others and promotes civility.

AUDIENCE

The primary audience for this book is educational technology coordinators, school librarians, health teachers and counselors, community mental health professionals who work in schools, and law enforcement officers who work with schools. Ultimately, the objective is that all content teachers will gain sufficient insight to effectively integrate instruction into the learning moments that arise. However, this initial team of professionals must assume the leadership in planning for the delivery of this instruction, as well as the bulk of the direct instruction. Having older students consult with this team is also important.

The reason this multidisciplinary team is important is because this situation is like the proverbial blind men trying to describe an elephant. These professionals have the expertise necessary to describe parts of the elephant but will have to work together to be able to see the entire elephant.

- Educational technology specialists have excellent understanding of the technologies and digital culture.
- School librarians have excellent insight into media literacy, which is an important foundation for all aspects of safe, ethical, and responsible online behavior.
- Counselors, health education teachers, and community mental health professionals understand effective youth risk prevention.
- School resource officers and other police officers can help students understand when activities may "cross the line" and involve criminal matters.
- Individuals with important expertise in these issues are walking around schools, likely wearing jeans and, when not in class, listening to iPods and texting friends.

The exciting thing is that when this recommended group of professionals and students talk about these issues, they will find an important commonality.

- Educational technology professionals and school librarians are embracing digital technologies as providing an exciting opportunity to shift to constructivist-based 21st-century instruction. They do not want to communicate messages about these technologies that are grounded in fear.
- Risk-prevention professionals understand effective risk-prevention messaging. They know that "scare tactics" approaches are ineffective and that the best way to prevent youth risk behavior is focus on positive social norms and youth skill building. Within this community, there is also awareness of the importance of encouraging positive actions of peers.
- The last thing students want to hear is fear messages.

PROTECTING CHILDREN IN THE 21ST CENTURY

The Protecting Children in the 21st Century Act added a provision to the Children's Internet Protection Act requiring that schools receiving E-Rate and other technology funds provide instruction in Internet safety.

As part of its Internet safety policy, the school must show that it is educating minors about appropriate online behavior, including interacting with other individuals on social networking websites and in chat rooms and cyberbullying awareness and response.[1]

Should instruction focus just on the Internet? For today's youth, this discussion must include all digital technologies. With today's cell phones, there is essentially little difference. It is all digital—and all about sharing and interacting.

Is this just about safety? Some of the issues that need to be addressed do relate to safety. But the discussion must be more comprehensive, addressing the interrelated aspects of safety and civility.

The focus of this book is on students in intermediate, middle, and high school grades. By the time young people turn thirteen, they are considered to be capable of engaging in most online activities, other than those specifically limited to adults. Many children lie about their age and enter the general digital world. Thus, by early middle school at the very latest, young people must be prepared to handle most of the safety concerns. Comprehensive coverage of issues related to sexual and personal relationships, however, can be delayed until later in middle school or high school.

A Cyber Savvy website has been set up to support this book at http://embracingdigitalyouth.org. This site provides access to surveys that can be used to support the instructional and evaluation activities suggested in this book, as well as stories and news articles that can be used to stimulate student discussions and a teacher's forum.

---

[1] 47 U.S.C. § 254(h)(5)(B)(iii).

Acknowledgments

If I started to thank everyone who has contributed to my expanding expertise in this area, I would unfortunately leave someone out. So I will thank instead a group.

About two years ago, I started a private online discussion group that has focused on youth risk online. This group has brought together researchers, risk prevention professionals, law enforcement, educators, industry, and others in a multidisciplinary collaborative online community. This group is seeking to address these issues and concerns in a manner that is grounded in accurate insight into the concerns, incorporates positive and effective risk prevention approaches, and is focused on engaging and empowering young people. Thus, I acknowledge all members of this group for their helpful insight and valuable discussions.

And thanks to my three children, who have provided me with ample "teachable moments" as they have grown.

Publisher's Acknowledgments

Corwin would like to thank the following individuals for taking the time to provide their editorial insight and guidance:

Aimée M. Bissonette, Attorney
Little Buffalo Law & Consulting
Minneapolis, Minnesota

Lori L. Grossman, Academic Trainer
Professional Development
Houston Independent School
    District
Houston, TX

Rose Cherie Reissman
NYC DOE Literacy Consultant IS62
Chief Executive Officer, Mind Lab
New York City, NY

Christopher Wells, Director
IT Policies and Communications
Gwinnett County Public Schools
Suwanee, GA

About the Author

Nancy Willard brings a varied background to the issues addressed in *Cyber Savvy: Embracing Digital Safety and Civility*.

She has degrees in elementary and special education and has taught students who presented serious emotional and behavioral problems. She also has a law degree and worked with computer technology companies. In the early 90s, she worked on projects that led to the establishment of the Oregon Public Education Network, the statewide Internet network for Oregon students.

In the mid-90s, she began to focus on issues of students' responsible use of the Internet and the more serious concerns of online aggression, abuse, and exploitation — work that has continued to this day.

In 2007, her pioneering book, *Cyberbullying and Cyberthreats: Responding to the Challenge of Online Social Cruelty, Threats, and Distress*, was published by Research Press. In that same year, a book for parents, *Cyber Safe Kids, Cyber Savvy Teens: Helping Young People Learn to Use the Internet in a Safe and Responsible Manner*, was published by Jossey-Bass.

Nancy is the mother of three and lives in Eugene, Oregon.

Part I

Teaching Digital Safety and Civility

Let Them Teach Each Other to Swim

WHAT DOES IT MEAN TO BE CYBER SAVVY?

The objective of *Cyber Savvy: Embracing Digital Safety and Civility* is to ensure that young people become savvy. *Savvy* comes from Latin *sapere*, meaning "to be wise"—astute, well informed, capable, perceptive, intelligent, discerning. All of these are words we would like to be able to apply to students when they are using digital technologies.

Being Cyber Savvy has four components. Cyber Savvy young people

1. *Keep themselves safe.* They understand the risks, and they know how to avoid getting into risky situations, to detect whether they are at risk, and to effectively respond to risk, including asking for help.
2. *Present a positive image.* They present themselves online as persons who make positive choices.
3. *Respect others.* They respect the rights, privacy, and property of others and treat others with civility.
4. *Take responsibility for the well-being of others.* They help others and report serious concerns to a responsible adult.

TEACH THEM TO SWIM

In the early 2000s, the major Internet safety concern was youth access to online pornography. Filtering software was promoted as the solution. The National Academy of Sciences (NAS) convened a task force that produced an excellent report, titled *Youth, Pornography and the Internet*.[1] An important statement from the preface of this report is the following:

> Swimming pools can be dangerous for children. To protect them, one can install locks, put up fences, and deploy pool alarms. All of these measures are helpful, but by far the most important thing that one can do for one's children is to teach them to swim.[2]

Yes, we need to teach young people to swim. Teaching them to swim safely and responsibly is even more important now that young people are all swimming around in the social networking "pool." If only it were that easy. It is exceptionally difficult to effectively teach young people to swim if

- they can't jump into a swimming pool at school because it is considered too risky;
- adults only know how to paddle in the shallow part of the pool or are afraid to get wet; and
- despite the fact that they have grown up in the water and may have excellent swimming skills, they are constantly warned that water is dangerous and filled with sharks.

Most adults have good insight into the risks and concerns associated with real life. When it comes to addressing the risks and concerns associated with use of digital technologies, it is necessary to deal with the challenge of the digital divide between *digital immigrants* and *digital natives*.

Young people are cruising down the information superhighway with their accelerators fully engaged, but sometimes without sufficient braking power, while many adults are struggling to get out of first gear. The situation is similar to that faced by immigrant parents who come to a new country. The children are readily able to acculturate to their new culture. Parents frequently struggle to accommodate.

There is a change in paradigm. In the old paradigm, adults understood the risks and the environment. Adults were generally in a position where they could detect risky behavior and intervene. Adults were the voice of authority. As digital immigrants, they are likely not to have significant credibility in the eyes of young people. Teachers who try to be "sages on the stage" are likely to trip on their togas.[3]

---

[1] Thornbourgh, D., & Lin, H. S. (Eds.) (2002). *Youth, pornography and the Internet*. Washington, DC: National Academy Press. Retrieved June 22, 2011, from http://www.nap.edu/openbook.php?isbn=0309082749

[2] Id., Preface.

[3] Borrowing language from King, A. (1993). Sage on the stage to guide on the side. *College Teaching, 41*(1), 30–35.

A constructive education approach—an environment where students gain insight through collaborative problem-solving interactions with peers—is essential. Teachers shift to being "guides on the side." To do so effectively, teachers must also have the necessary insight into the issues to be effective guides.

The focus of this book is in accord with the NAS statement, but with a slight twist. We must recognize that students do not want to drown or see others drown, and many already have excellent swimming skills. Therefore, we must strive to ensure all students gain top-notch swimming skills by setting up situations where they can teach each other to swim—under the guidance of a savvy adult.

RISKS AND BENEFITS OF DIGITAL TECHNOLOGIES

Numerous research studies document that the majority of young people make positive choices when using digital technologies, demonstrate effective skills in responding to the negative incidents that occur, and are generally not excessively distressed by these negative incidents. Online risk does not necessarily equal harm.[4] Furthermore, we cannot expect that young people will never have to deal with a negative incident. Negative incidents are a naturally occurring part of life.

The situation is equivalent to riding a bicycle.[5] There are clearly risks associated with riding a bicycle, as well as significant benefits. There are risks, as well as benefits, associated with communicating with people online who are not known in person. Therefore, just as we teach young people the possible risks they face when riding a bicycle and what they need to do to keep themselves safe, we need to ensure that young people know the risks when communicating online with someone whom they do not know in person—and how to do so safely.

Research has also demonstrated that the young people who are at the greatest risk online appear to be the ones who are at greater risk generally.[6] They demonstrate other psychosocial concerns, along with other risk

---

[4]Berkman Internet Safety Technical Task Force. (2008). *Enhancing child safety and online technologies. Appendix C: Literature review from the Research Advisory Board.* Retrieved June 22, 2011, from http://cyber.law.harvard.edu/sites/cyber.law.harvard.edu/files/ISTTF_Final_Report-APPENDIX_C_TF_Project_Plan.pdf; Collier, A., & Nigam, H. (2010, June 4). *Youth safety on a living Internet* (Report of the Online Safety and Technology Working Group). National Telecommunications and Information Administration, p. 25. Retrieved June 22, 2011, from http://www.ntia.doc.gov/reports/2010/OSTWG_Final_Report_060410.pdf

[5]Livingstone, S., Haddon, L., Görzig, A., & Ólafsson, K. (2011). *Risks and safety on the internet: The perspective of European children.* Full Findings (EU Kids Online). London: LSE. Retrieved June 22, 2011, from http://www2.lse.ac.uk/media@lse/research/EUKidsOnline/Home.aspx

[6]Berkman Internet Safety Technical Task Force, supra; Collier & Nigam, supra.

behaviors. Thus, digital risk behavior appears not to be new risk behavior; rather, this is youth risk behavior that is now manifesting through the use of digital technologies.

Use of interactive digital technologies can change the dynamics of risk behavior—as well as provide positive benefits.

- Materials captured in digital format can be widely disseminated and permanently available. This may cause greater harm to self or others, but it may also provide the opportunity for early detection and personal accountability.
- Young people can achieve greater invisibility. This may encourage risky or irresponsible behavior. This can also allow them to more easily find prevention information and obtain assistance from online support sites.
- Use of technologies may sometimes interfere with the recognition of harmful consequences to self or others. This can interfere with empathy and responsible decision making. However, this may increase the ability of young people to more effectively predict negative consequences because they are required to do so more frequently.
- Young people are interacting with increasing numbers of people online. Some people may be less safe, and it can be harder to detect possible risk. Marginalized youth may also find important acceptance and support from online friends who share their more unique interests.

FOUNDATION OF CYBER SAVVY APPROACH

The overall focus of this book is on the need to do the following:

Proceed in a Multidisciplinary Manner

It will not be possible to address these new concerns if professionals remain in "silos." Many times, these issues are grounded in mental concerns or lead to mental health concerns. Off-campus actions can seriously affect schools. Sometimes young people are criminally victimized or engage in criminal acts. It will take the proverbial village to effectively address these concerns.

Ensure Scientific Integrity

Initiatives must be grounded in an accurate understanding of the risks and resulting harm, risk factors, and protective factors. Many times, the statistics related to youth risk online, as reported in the press, have been derived from studies that lack academic rigor, fail to provide adequate definitions, or fail to effectively distinguish between more minor incidents that young people have effectively resolved and the more serious incidents. Such reports have, at times, created a misperception about the degree and manner of risk. We also lack a full understanding of these issues because research insight is still emerging.

Implement Innovative Initiatives That Have a Likelihood of Success

There are no evidence-based best practices to guide the implementation of instruction, prevention, and intervention initiatives. Research insight into these risks is still emerging. The ever-changing technology environment presents barriers to achieving a broadly applicable understanding of concerns and the implementation of stable prevention and intervention initiatives. We do not have the luxury of waiting for systematic empirical research that provides evidence of statistically significant effectiveness in prevention and intervention.

Thus, there is a need to shift to approaches that are grounded in what we know from current research and about effective risk prevention. Innovative initiatives must ensure accountability and the likelihood of success through ongoing evaluation and attention to emerging research—and modification when necessary, as informed by this research and evaluation.

Engage and Empower Youth

Young people engage in online environments where frequently there are no reasonable adults present. Use of mobile technologies significantly interferes with adult supervision. Many research studies document that young people often do not report negative situations involving technologies to adults.[7] Thus, we must focus on increasing the ability of all young people to be safe, encourage civility, engage in effective conflict resolution, and know how and when they should report significant concerns to adults.

CYBER SAVVY APPROACH

The Cyber Savvy approach is grounded in these critical components.

- Reinforce positive social norms and practices.
- Foster effective problem solving and the use of effective strategies.
- Empower and engage witnesses to be helpful allies.
- Collect local data to guide instruction and support ongoing evaluation.

---

[7] Berkman Internet Safety Technical Task Force, supra, p. 44.

Positive Social Norms and Practices

Stan Davis, author of *Schools Where Everybody Belongs* (2005) and *Empowering Bystanders* (2007), provided the following sage guidance related to bullying prevention:

We can build positive actions by peers who are aware of mean behavior through these interventions:

- Survey youth to determine which mean behaviors they see and hear about, which behaviors they would like to see adults take action about, whether they believe peers should report these behaviors, and whether they believe peers should take action to support others.
- Use survey results to shape positive peer actions through peer-norming interventions. Help young people see that most of their peers share their dislike of mean behaviors and their belief that they should take positive actions to stop the negative impact of these behaviors.
- In addition, use those survey results to identify needs for interventions to build awareness of the negative impact of some mean behaviors.
- Help youth to build a diverse repertoire of positive actions to take when they are aware of mean behavior. These actions should include alliance building, in which youth connect with peers who also disapprove of mean behavior. These actions should include a wide range of supportive behaviors for the person mistreated, including face-to-face support, support in the digital world, and other ways to let the mistreated person know he or she is not alone. The actions should include ways to ask adult resources for help and to express standards for digital civility.
- Provide young people with opportunities to practice a wide range of positive actions in response to mean behavior.
- Build awareness among youth that they have an obligation as citizens of their school, physical community, and digital community to protect the safety and well-being of other citizens, even those who are not their friends.[8]

---

[8] Stan provided this guidance in the context of a preconference workshop on Youth Risk Online, presented on November 15, 2010, at the International Bullying Prevention Association Conference in Seattle, Washington.

Stan's guidance is in accord with a research-based approach used by Drs. Perkins and Craig who direct the Youth Health and Safety project.[9] Their approach with schools on bullying prevention programs is as follows:

> The social norms approach to preventing problem behavior and promoting and reinforcing positive behavior, put simply, is to dispel the myths about the problem being the norm among peers. It starts with gathering credible data from a population and identifying the actual norms regarding the attitudes and behavior of concern. Then a social norms intervention intensively communicates the truth through media campaigns, interactive programs, personalized normative feedback, and other educational venues. Evidence has shown youth and adults responding to these initiatives with more realistic perceptions of positive peer norms lead to decreases in problem behavior and increases in positive behavior in the population.[10]

This approach is exactly what we need to do to address the concerns of digital safety and civility. Simply rewrite Davis' statement, substituting "unsafe or hurtful digital behavior" for the term "mean behavior."

Imagine the effectiveness of student-created posters or screen savers, "public service announcements," or other presentations made to like-aged students, younger students, or parents with statements like

- 90 percent of (name of school) students have set their social networking profile to "friends only";
- 85 percent of (name of school) students only friend people whom they know in person and trust on their social networking profile;
- 78 percent of (name of school) students would feel comfortable showing all of the photos they have posted in their social networking profile to a teacher;
- 87 percent of (name of school) students think that students should not post hurtful comments about other students online, send mean text messages, or share personal information or a photo that has been sent privately; and
- 98 percent of (name of school) students think it is very dangerous to send a nude photo to anyone.

---

[9] Perkins, W., Craig, D., & Perkins, J. (2009, November 10). Misperceptions of bullying norms as a risk factor associated with violence among middle school students. Paper presented at the American Public Health Association Annual Meeting, Philadelphia, PA. Retrieved June 22, 2011, from http://www.youthhealthsafety.org/

[10] Id.

Imagine you are teaching a class on cyberbullying and have conducted a survey that asked students whether they want to be friends with someone who sends hurtful messages to people, posts hurtful material online that denigrates others, or will distribute information or photos sent privately to others—and the overwhelming majority of students have indicated that they would not want to be friends with a person who does this. The survey could also ask them to describe the words that they would use to describe someone who will publicly protest if someone is posting hurtful material about another student—and the responses to this survey included "Leader!" "Awesome!" "Superstar!" "Hero!" and "Brave and trustworthy!" How would this impact their helper behavior?

The Cyber Savvy approach also focuses on the reasons or rationale for such norms. Not only should we be focusing attention on what the majority of students think about these issues; it is also helpful for students to enunciate why. When asked "Why?" the responses will focus on consequences—the desire either to achieve positive outcomes or to avoid negative ones. Additionally, the surveys solicit information on the strategies used to respond to negative incidents and the effectiveness of those strategies. All of this student-based insight can be turned into instructional messaging.

Surveys can be conducted on sites like Survey Monkey.[11] The raw anonymous data can be provided to the students to enable them to engage in analysis. Students will likely find an analysis of what they think incredibly fascinating. This analysis will reinforce their values and skills, and influence the thinking of those students whose rationale is found by the majority to be lacking in insight. This will also communicate a strong message that important adults in their lives respect their values and skills. Using older students to communicate these messages to younger students is an approach that is strongly recommended. These are all powerful social influence strategies.

The next important task is to translate these positive norms into messaging:

- Personal statements of positive standards
- Posters or screen savers that communicate these norms to all
- Audio or video "public service announcements" that can be played at their school and for younger students
- Slide presentations that can be made to fellow students, younger students, or parents
- Press releases sent to local news media
- Presentations at a school board meeting

---

[11] http://www.surveymonkey.com/

Problem Solving and Use of Effective Strategies

Sometimes young people make mistakes; they may engage in risky behavior or get angry and lash out inappropriately—and sometimes they are harmed by others. Because they are teens and their brains are still under development, they biologically do not have the capacity to consistently make effective decisions. Frequently, they are impulsive, failing to think about the possible consequences of their actions. They lack the range of experience that adults have in understanding and negotiating human relationships, especially those that involve some risk or altercations. Lastly, there are aspects of the digital environment that can interfere with effective problem solving.

Repeated research studies also demonstrate that a significant majority of teens do not tell adults about negative incidents that occur when using digital technologies.[12] While sometimes they do not report problems because they fear adult overreaction, many times they don't report because they have already fixed the problem—or they perceive that they ought to be able to fix the problem. It is not developmentally appropriate for teens to always tell adults about their problems. An important life task in the teen years is learning how to take care of your own problems. Just as a toddler who needs to learn how to walk will protest being carried even when challenged by stairs or uneven surfaces, teens will try to resolve difficult situations on their own because this is the only way they can learn how effectively resolve difficult situations.

Thus, an important approach is to provide them with the insight and skills they need to effectively resolve their own problems. An excellent social-emotional learning program for middle school students is Second Step, by Committee for Children.[13] Second Step is a comprehensive program that focuses on empathy and communication, bullying prevention, and problem solving. The problem-solving steps are incorporated throughout the lessons, just as they should be in teaching digital safety and civility. The Second Step problem-solving steps are as follows:

1. Analyze the situation.
2. Brainstorm options.

---

[12] Wolak, J., Mitchell, K., & Finkelhor, D. (2006). *Online victimization of youth: Five years later* (National Center for Missing & Exploited Children Bulletin 07-06-025). Alexandria, VA: National Center for Missing & Exploited Children. Retrieved June 22, 2011, from http://www.unh.edu/ccrc/pdf/CV138 .pdf; McQuade, S. C., & Sampat, N. (2008). *Study of Internet and at risk behaviors.* Rochester Institute of Technology Center for Multidisciplinary Studies. Retrieved June 22, 2011, from http://www .rrcsei.org/RIT%20Cyber%20Survey%20Final%20Report.pdf; Follaco, J. (2008, June 18). "Startling new reality" of cybercrime revealed in RIT research. *PRWeb.* Retrieved June 22, 2011, from http:// www.prweb.com/releases/Cyber_Safety/Ethics_Initiative/prweb1035784.htm; Livingston et al., supra.

[13] http://www.cfchildren.org/programs/ssp/overview/

3. Consider each option.
4. Decide on and do the best option.
5. Evaluate if it works.
6. Figure out another way (*if necessary*).

Unfortunately, it is well known that young people are more apt to engage in impulsive actions that skip over this kind of analysis. When they make impulsive decisions, teens appear to be more inclined to act in accordance with what they think their peers think or would do. Thus, there is a connection between social norms and decision making. If they know in advance what the positive peer norms and effective strategies in these situations are, they will hopefully be less inclined to engage in an impulsive action that is contrary to these positive practices and strategies.

This situation is complicated further because their decision making is now heavily influenced by the fact that they are acting within a digital environment. This is discussed in Chapter 2. Assist students in developing very effective problem-solving and decision-making skills within the digital environment by focusing their attention on the permanence and potential wide distribution of the digital materials that demonstrate evidence of their decision making, either positively or negatively.

Empowering and Engaging Witnesses

The importance of the role of witnesses when addressing these issues cannot be overstated.[14] So many times, when young people are engaging in risk behavior, harming others, or being harmed, there are no responsible adults present. Risk-prevention approaches that rely on increased adult surveillance, like preventing bullying by increasing hallway supervision, are not adaptable to this new environment. Influencing positive witness responses and reporting is critically important. When young people witness negative situation, they essentially have the choice of three paths:

1. Hurtful participant
2. Passive observer
3. Helpful ally

Insight into strategies for how to encourage students to be helpful allies comes from the work of Eva Fogelman, a historian, psychotherapist, and second-generation survivor of the Holocaust who conducted

---

[14] Davis, S., & Davis, J. (2007). *Empowering bystanders in bullying prevention.* Champaign, IL: Research Press.

interviews with "rescuers" during Hitler's reign.[15] Fogelman identified four factors that appeared to set the stage for the willingness of someone to be a rescuer. These factors have been outlined as follows:

> [F]irst, well developed inner values, which came from deep in childhood, that stressed acceptance of difference in others, a conviction that individual action matters, and religious or moral convictions that supported those values. . . . [S]econd, a loving home, reasoned and firm guidance in childhood, a model of altruistic behavior in the person of a caregiver or other authoritative adult, practice at thinking and acting independently of the opinion of others, and a serious illness or death in one's family. . . . [T]hird, a strong sense of one's own competency to find creative solutions to very difficult problems and to handle the secrecy, fear, and terror of rescue. . . . [A]nd fourth, "channel factors" and an "enabling situation," that is, the availability of a safe hiding place, of someone to request the rescuer's help, of a potential victim who could "pass," of food, and of a support organization to provide ration cards, counterintelligence, money, etc. Sympathy was not enough; the timing had to be right.[16]

Encourage students to engage in proactive helping behaviors.

- Reinforce the importance and leadership status of those who step up to ensure the well-being of others.
- Make sure they fully understand the potential harmful consequences that could result to others.
- In the context of discussions of possible or actual scenarios, provide practice in effective helping skills.

Ongoing Evaluation

The key to the effective implementation of the Cyber Savvy approach is to regularly conduct surveys of the students in your schools using a web-based survey tool. The Cyber Savvy surveys, available at http://embracingdigitalyouth.org assess the following aspects:

- Negative incidents and degree of distress—the number of incidents, as well as the degree to which the incident caused distress

---

[15] Fogelman, E. (1994). *Conscience and courage: Rescuers of Jews during the Holocaust.* New York, NY: Anchor Books.

[16] Blumenthal, D. (1994). Review of E. Fogelman, *Conscience and courage: Rescuers of Jews during the Holocaust. Journal of Psychology and Theology,* 23, 62–63. Retrieved June 22, 2011, from http://www.js.emory.edu/BLUMENTHAL/Fogelman.html

and for how long, are important information. For needs assessment, this information will provide insight into the concerns that are being faced by your students. For evaluation after prevention education and interventions, the percentage of students who are involved in negative incidents and the degree of distress should decrease.

- Strategies used and degree of effectiveness—how students are responding to negative incidents and how effective these responses are. This includes self-help actions and situations where the student has asked a peer or an adult for assistance. For instruction purposes, identifying effective strategies used by students will have a powerful influence on the inclination of other students to adopt such strategies. For evaluation, reviewing data collected later can reveal whether the instruction has increased the usage of effective strategies.

- Norms, practices, and rationale—instructionally, this data is used for positive norms messaging. In subsequent surveys for evaluation, the percentage of students reporting positive norms and practices should increase.

INSTRUCTIONAL OPPORTUNITIES

Opportunities to provide instruction addressing issues of digital safety and civility include the following:

- *Provide direct instruction.* This can include a review of provisions of the district's Internet use policy, instruction in technology or library classes, addressing the more significant risks in health education classes, and direct instruction opportunities in student homerooms or advisories.

- *Integrate digital safety and civility concepts into other instruction.* These opportunities will become more available as schools transition into greater use of interactive Web 2.0 technologies for instruction.

- *Use "teachable moments."* Use incidents and news stories as opportunities to focus on actual consequences. This approach includes especially appropriate activities for homerooms or student advisories.

- *Provide informal instruction.* This might include posters, hints on the computer screen, public service announcements, and the like.

CYBER SAVVY OBJECTIVES

Part II of this book will provide readers with in-depth information on the key issues that must be addressed to ensure that young people are engaging in safe, positive, respectful, and responsible behavior when using digital technologies. The overall objectives fall into the following categories:

Avoid the Impulse

- Remember, what you do reflects on you.
  - If you engage in an impulsive negative act that results in posting or sending material in digital format, this material can become widely disseminated and possibly permanently available. This could harm your reputation, friendships, and opportunities; place you at risk; or cause harm to others.
  - Engage in effective problem solving and positive decision making before posting or sending anything. Be a helpful ally if you see someone is at risk or is being harmed.

Read With Your Eyes Open

- Assess the credibility of information.
  - Anyone can post or send anything online, and there is no guarantee that what has been posted or sent is accurate. Individuals, organizations, and companies may use sophisticated techniques to seek to influence your attitudes and behavior.
  - Carefully assess the credibility of all information accessed on websites or received in messages and the trustworthiness of people you interact with.

Keep Your Life in Balance

- Avoid addictive use of digital technologies.
  - While use of digital technologies can be fun and allow you to connect with your friends, excessive use of digital technologies can be unhealthy.
  - Ensure your use of digital technologies does not interfere with other activities that will make your life happy and successful.

(Continued)

(Continued)

Think Before You Post

- Protect your reputation and respect others.
  - Other people will judge your character and decision making based on the material you post and send. This can effect your reputation, friendships, and opportunities positively or negatively. You can hurt others if you post or send material that reveals their personal information.
  - Be careful whenever posting or sending material in digital format. Respect the rights and privacy of others.

Connect Safely

- Interact safely with others online.
  - You will interact with many different people online. Most are safe and trustworthy, but some may not be. It is easier for people to be deceitful and manipulative online.
  - Be careful when you interact with people online. Only let people you know, or those whom your good friends know, have access to your personal profile. If you want to meet in person with someone you have gotten to know online, make a safe meeting plan and bring along friends.

Keep Yourself Secure

- Implement security and avoid scams.
  - Digital technologies can be corrupted with malware, which often is used to commit identity theft. Criminals use the Internet to commit a variety of scams.
  - Ensure your computer security is maintained and your activities do not increase your risk. Watch out for scams—offers that are too good to be true or threaten loss if you do not share personal information.

Abide by the Terms

- Act in accord with policies, terms, and laws.
  - Your online activities are governed by laws, use policies of the organization that provides your access, and the terms

of use of the websites or services. These laws, policies, and terms ensure that user's activities do not cause harm to others or to the technical system.
  o Follow the standards to protect the rights of everyone.

Stay Out of the Garbage

- Avoid objectionable and illegal material.
  o People distribute materials online that are harmful to others, including pornographic material. You could accidentally access this material. Accessing or distributing child pornography is a serious crime.
  o Use safe surfing techniques to avoid accidentally accessing this material. Know how to effectively respond if such material is accidentally accessed. Don't access or distribute child pornography.

Don't Sell Yourself

- Disclose and consume wisely.
  o The financial model of the Internet involves providing access to free content and services in exchange for market profiling and advertising. Sites and apps track your postings and activities to create a market profile that guides the advertisements you will see. Social networking sites encourage friends to send advertisements to their friends. You can find helpful information about companies and their produces or services online.
  o Make a personal decision about how much personal information you want to share with sites and apps. Use the Internet to research companies, products, and services prior to making purchases.

Protect Your Face and Friends

- Be savvy and civil when networking.
  o Social networking sites are fun places to post information and connect with friends but present risks that involve posting inappropriate material or engaging in unsafe interactions with others. These sites encourage users to share personal information and have many friends

(Continued)

(Continued)

so they and their advertisers can obtain market profile information and use friendship connections to encourage purchasing. The terms of use prohibit hurtful actions.

○ Protect your privacy by limiting access to your profile to those you have friended. Protect your reputation and respect others when you post. Friend only people whom you or a trusted friend know in person. Report abuse.

Embrace Civility

● Prevent hurtful digital communications.

○ The vast majority of people do not like to see others post hurtful material, send hurtful messages, disclose private material, or cause other harm through digital communications.

○ Exercise care when posting or sending material so you do not place yourself at risk of attack. If someone is hurting you, wait until you have calmed down to respond. Save the evidence. Then calmly tell the person to stop, ignore or block the communications, or file an abuse report—or all three. If the person does not stop, ask for help. Recognize that no one deserves to be attacked online. If you hurt others, this will damage your reputation and friendships. If you see someone being harmed, provide support to that person and speak up against the harm. If the situation is serious or continues, report to a responsible adult.

Cyberdate Safely

● Avoid exploitation and abusive relationships.

○ Watch out for fantasy relationships.

– Recognize that forming close personal relationships primarily through digital technologies can lead to unrealistic understandings and expectations.

– Proceed with caution when forming a relationship digitally.

○ Avoid exploitation.

– People you communicate with online may try to exploit you sexually by asking for nude photos or seeking sexual encounters. They may be online strangers or people you know—adults or other teens. Sexual relations between adults and teens are illegal. Common grooming techniques involve sending overly friendly messages and being overly eager to establish a close relationship. If you send a nude photo to anyone, that person could, at any time, distribute the photo to everyone, and your reputation will be trashed or the person could use that photo to blackmail you.

- If someone appears to be trying to manipulate you to engage in sexual activities or requests a nude photo, discontinue contact and report this to an adult.

o Do not allow a partner to abuse you.

- An abusive partner may try to use digital technologies to control you by constantly texting and controlling your digital communications with others.
- Do not allow a partner to seek to control you in this manner.

Making Positive Choices Online

To effectively influence students to make positive choices requires understanding some of the developmental factors and influences—negative or positive—that are implicated in making decisions when using digital technologies. Researchers have identified a phenomenon that is sometimes called *disinhibition* to describe the idea that sometimes, when people are using digital technologies, they do things they would not normally do in the real world.[1]

By understanding the factors that could influence behavior when using digital technologies, it is possible to help students recognize when their actions might be influenced in a negative direction and to implement strategies that will reinforce the influences for positive behavior.

The insight in this section draws from the social learning theory, specifically Bandura's theory on moral disengagement.[2] According to this theory, people may turn off their inclination to engage in what they believe to be appropriate moral standards of behavior. But when they do so, they create rationalizations or justifications for why failing to abide by these standards is necessary or required in this particular situation.

Bandura has identified four major ways in which the motivation to engage in responsible actions can be disengaged. These include

---

[1] Suler, J. (2004). The online disinhibition effect. *CyberPsychology and Behavior, 7*: 321–326. Retrieved June 22, 2011, from http://www-usr.rider.edu/~suler/psycyber/disinhibit.html

[2] Bandura, A. (1991). Social cognition theory of moral thought and action. In W. M. Kurtines & J. L. Gewirtz (Eds.), *Handbook of moral behavior and development* (Vol. 1, pp. 45–96). Hillsdale, NJ: Lawrence Erlbaum.

- *Reconstruing conduct.* Actions are portrayed as serving some larger purpose, such as supporting a friend; or euphemistic phrases are used to describe the action, such as "I was just playing around."
- *Displacing or diffusing responsibility.* This can occur if someone else can be blamed for "requiring" or "requesting" the action or if many people are engaging in certain behavior, so no one person appears to be responsible.
- *Disregarding or misrepresenting injurious consequences.* Sometimes the perception that the harm was minimal is balanced against the benefit received.
- *Dehumanizing or blaming the victim.* Once the victim has been dehumanized or blamed for what has happened, it is easier to rationalize that the actions taken were justified.

What should become evident is the degree to which use of digital technologies can interfere with the recognition that actions have resulted in a harmful consequence—and the diffusion of personal responsibility if a person believes his or her actions are invisible.

The following material builds on Bandura's work by identifying factors that appear to be interfering with responsible decision making when using technologies, as well as by discussing the countervailing factors that could influence more positive behavior.

DEVELOPMENTAL CHALLENGES

Didn't Think: Brain Development

Children lack sufficient brain development to independently make good choices online. If they still believe in such fanciful creatures as Santa Claus and the tooth fairy, they simply do not have the brain-development capacity to comprehend how the Internet works. Therefore, for children, it is necessary to seek to educate parents about how they can set up a "safer playground" online. Protective technologies can be used effectively with children to do this. These protective technologies can assist in making sure children only access the sites and communicate with people their parents have approved. Primary grade students should learn simple guidelines for safety within these protected environments.

A teenager's frontal cortex, which supports rational, ethical decision making, is undergoing significant development.[3] Learning to make good

---

[3] National Institute of Mental Health. (2001). *Teenage brain: A work in progress (fact sheet)* (NIH Publication No. 01-4929). Retrieved June 22, 2011, from http://www.nimh.nih.gov/health/publications/teenage-brain-a-work-in-progress.shtml

decisions requires practice and paying attention to the consequences of actions. Teens appear to process emotions in the "fight or flight" region of brain. So if emotions are involved, teens may be even less able to think things through and make good decisions than usual.

Use of digital technologies can interfere with effective problem solving because it can be more difficult to gain a full understanding of the situation or to recognize the harmful consequences. Unfortunately, if young people post or send material when they are upset, this can result in damaging material being widely disseminated.

Teens are also biologically compelled to want to make their own decisions, because this is how they develop the capacity to effectively do so. Many teens do not report negative incidents that have occurred online because they want to be able to resolve these situations by themselves.[4]

Help preteens and teens learn to engage in effective problem solving. Make sure students know that if they are emotionally upset, they are much more likely to make mistakes, and therefore the best choice is to avoid posting or sending material when upset.

Who Am I? Exploration of Identity

Eric Erickson's pioneering work outlined that the primary task during adolescence is figuring out who you are.[5] To do this, teens must engage in exploration and try out new ways of thinking and behaving. They will explore new ways of looking, new ideas, and new groups of friends. In the context of these explorations, teens will eventually commit to their own personal identity.

Social networking profiles have become a public venue for teens to explore their emerging personal identity.[6] For better or worse, this makes their explorations of self far more visible, and potentially enduring, because evidence of their explorations may be permanently available.

Some teens may experiment with new personal identities by establishing a *false persona*—a profile that presents an image of them that is not consistent with real life. The "avatars" young people produce in gaming sites also provide ways to express different personalities.

Encourage young people to present a strong positive image online and to evaluate others based on what they post. Encourage teens to use profile creation as a way to reflect on how they want others to see them. Share news stories of situations where a person's reputation and opportunities were damaged based on the material posted online.

---

[4] Wolak et al. (2006), supra; Juvonen, J., & Gross, E. F. (2008). Extending the school grounds? Bullying experiences in cyberspace. *Journal of School Health, 78*, 496–505.

[5] Erikson, E. (1968). *Identity, youth and crisis.* New York, NY: W. W. Norton.

[6] Boyd, D. (2007). Why youth (heart) social network sites: The role of networked publics in teenage social life. In D. Buckingham (Ed.), *Youth, identity, and digital media* (MacArthur Foundation Series on Digital Learning) (pp. 119–142). Cambridge, MA: MIT Press. Retrieved June 22, 2011, from www.danah.org/papers/WhyYouthHeart.pdf

Am I Hot? Maturing Sexuality and Exploring Personal Relationships

Teens are maturing sexually, and this maturation includes both physical and emotional changes. Media and advertising often promote provocative sexuality, communicating how important it is to be "hot."[7] Unfortunately, media and advertising can be a strong influence on how teens present themselves and judge others.

Teens can find appropriate and helpful information and support about their sexuality online, or they may find unhealthy photos and information. Teens are also exploring personal relationships digitally. This can deepen personal relationships in a very healthy manner or can result in manipulation and exploitation. It appears that a significant amount of cyberbullying, especially at the high school level, is tied to maturing sexuality and personal relationships.

Address these issues in the context of comprehensive sex education.

INFLUENCES: NEGATIVE OR POSITIVE

Visibility Factors

You Can't See Me: Perception of Invisibility

The degree to which your actions might be visible to others, especially people in a position of authority, has always been a factor in guiding decision making. The perception of invisibility, or ability to achieve anonymity, can remove concerns of detection, which could lead to disapproval or punishment. Plato's story "The Ring of Gyges" tells a story of a shepherd who finds a ring. When the stone is turned to the inside, the wearer becomes invisible.[8] Thus, a very long time ago, Plato was raising the question of how people may choose to act if they perceive themselves to be invisible.

It is possible to establish a high degree of invisibility using digital technologies. For example, someone can easily create a fake profile on Facebook or use an anonymous e-mail service. People can also be quite invisible in chat rooms and on gaming sites.

There are risks and benefits to this invisibility. People may use the ability to achieve invisibility online to engage in hurtful behavior. However, invisibility can be beneficial to a teen who is facing a significant challenge because this teen may feel safer seeking support on an online support service site if he or she cannot be identified.

---

[7] American Psychological Association. (2007). *Report of the APA Task Force on the sexualization of girls.* Washington, DC: Author. Retrieved June 22, 2011, from http://www.apa.org/pi/wpo/sexualization .html

[8] Ring of Gyges. (n.d.). In *Wikipedia.* Retrieved June 22, 2011, from http://en.wikipedia.org/wiki/ Ring_of_Gyges

Everyone Can See Me: Visibility

The fact that everyone can see you is the opposite of "You Can't See Me." In the early days of the Internet, there was a cartoon in the *New Yorker* in which a dog is sitting at a computer talking to another dog, saying, "On the Internet, nobody knows you are a dog."[9] That was then—before social networking. With Web 2.0, not only does everyone know you are a dog but they also know what breed you are, who you run with, where your bones are buried, the accidental piddle behind the couch, the fight you got into with the boxer, and your thoughts on the hot poodle down the street.

Strategies

Emphasize that whatever students post on their social networking profiles can easily be seen by people whom they do not know even if they have strictly set their privacy settings. A friend could show what they have posted to anyone—another teen, a parent, or the principal. Remind them that any material sent privately in digital format to anyone, even a best friend, can easily go "viral." Ensure that students understand, however, that it is possible to trace wrongdoers because they always leave "digital footprints." Encourage involvement in less anonymous environments, because these are safer. Encourage them to act in accord with internalized values, regardless of whether they can be identified.

Consequences

I Can't See You: Lack of Tangible Feedback

As young people grow, they become better able to predict how others might feel, even if those others are not present.[10] They also become more skilled in predicting the possible consequences of actions and evaluating the motivations of others, which is critically important in learning how to make positive choices.

The lack of tangible feedback about consequences of online actions for others or for themselves can interfere with the recognition for teens that their actions have had a harmful consequence, which can interfere with empathy and may lead to a lack of remorse. This may also interfere with learning to engage in effective problem solving. The lack of tangible feedback can also make it more difficult to recognize when another person is being deceitful.

---

[9] From a famous cartoon by Peter Steiner, *The New Yorker*, July 5, 1993.

[10] Hoffman, M. L. (1991). Empathy, social cognition and moral action. In W. M. Kurtines & J. L. Gewirtz (Eds.), *Handbook of moral behavior and development* (Vol. 1, pp. 275–299). Hillsdale, NJ: Lawrence Erlbaum.

Do Unto Others: The Benefit of Mutual Benefits

The injunction to "do unto others . . ."—otherwise known as the Golden Rule—is grounded in the principle of reciprocity. A version of the Golden Rule is present in every religion and spiritual philosophy.[11] If you want people to treat you fairly, respect your rights, and not send you hurtful messages, it is a good idea to treat others fairly, respect their rights, and not send hurtful messages to them.

A fascinating concept to consider is how the principal of reciprocity might influence how groups of people function in situations where there is no apparent authority present. The World Wide Web is often compared to the Wild Wild West—a place of opportunity, freedom, and no rules. When the early pioneers traveled to the West, did they really enter into an environment of anarchy that resulted in lawlessness? In fact, not at all. The miners, cattlemen, trappers, and others who settled the West independently formed contracts and implemented dispute resolution approaches, all without reliance on any governmental body.[12] These contracts and resolution processes were grounded in mutual benefit—an agreement to abide by standards that respected the right of others. The apparent motivation was that these contracts would also protect their own interests.

The term *anarchy* comes from the Greek anarchía, which means "without ruler."[13] There are, interestingly, two very different interpretations of the meaning of this word: (1) state of lawlessness or political disorder due to the absence of governmental authority; (2) a utopian society of individuals who enjoy complete freedom without government. It would appear that the way to achieve a utopian society when authority is less evident is through mutual benefit agreements.

Strategies

Enhance the ability of students to predict how unseen others might feel and the consequences of actions. Make sure students know that if they do not know someone very well in real life, what they are told online, or even who this person is, could be deceptive. Focus their attention on how they would feel if someone did something like this to them. Expand this discussion to how they can form social norms for their own digital communities that are based on an agreement to abide by standards that are mutually beneficial for all members of the community.

---

[11] Shared belief on the "Golden Rule" (a/k/a. ethics of reciprocity). (2011, May 16). *ReligiousTolerance. org.* Retrieved June 22, 2011, from http://www.religioustolerance.org/reciproc.htm

[12] Anderson, T. L., & Hill, P. J. (2004). *The not so wild, wild west: Property rights on the frontier.* Stanford, CA: Stanford University Press.

[13] Anarchy. (2011). In *Merriam-Webster.com.* Retrieved June 22, 2011, from http://www.merriam-webster.com/dictionary/anarchy

Social Norms

Everybody Does It: Influence of Perceived Negative Norms

People are highly influenced by social norms—negatively or positively. The message that cyberbullying is an epidemic and that many teens engage in this hurtful behavior could be backfiring. If students believe that many young people send hurtful messages, then when they are angry with someone, they may decide it is perfectly appropriate to send a hurtful message—because "everybody does it." Unfortunately, there is a heavy influence on social networking sites for norms that support posting lots of information and friending many people because this supports market profiling and advertising; however, these norms may not be safe or wise.

Positive Is the Norm

In fact, everybody does not make negative choices or hurt others online, and the majority of people do not approve of or like this kind of behavior.[14] The majority of young people want to keep themselves safe, make positive choices, and respect others; and they are concerned about the well-being of others.

Strategies

Constantly remind students that people do not look favorably on those who make negative choices or are hurtful to others and that if they demonstrate negative choices or hurtful behavior in a digital environment, the significant visibility of those negative choices will provide evidence that could damage their reputation, friendships, and future opportunities. Encourage students to resist peer or commercial influence that is inconsistent with their personal values and standards. Encourage them to think of the norms they want to encourage within their digital communities. Help them be able to challenge digital social norms that support irresponsible behavior by focusing on the predictable harmful consequences of following such norms.

Standards

Because I Can, It Must Be Okay

The easy ability to engage in actions using digital technologies appears to support a decision that it must be okay to do so. "The easy

---

[14]HInduja, S., & Patchin, J. W. (2011, March 10). Overview of cyberbullying. Paper presented at the Whitehouse Conference on Bullying Prevention. Retrieved June 22, 2011, from http://www.stopbullying.gov/references/white_house_conference/index.html

ability to download copyrighted music or forward an embarrassing photo of someone, must mean this is okay," is the logic. Teens are also in a developmental time where they may test limits—and it seems easier to test these limits in a digital environment.

This factor sometimes works in conjunction with the invisibility factor. Not only is it easy to do something; but this can be done with a significant degree of invisibility, thus limiting possible detection and punishment. Other times, the perception that many are engaging in such actions, because they can, also contributes to the belief that it is okay.

Common Values Are Common for a Reason: Prevention of Harm

Many adults are inclined to try to send the message "Don't to this. You will be caught and punished." This argument is likely not highly effective in the digital environment, because it is too easy to become invisible or because of the perception that many are doing it. Thus, the risks of individual identification and punishment are low.

Strategy

Focus on common values and the reasons for those values. School and employer Internet-use policies, terms-of-use agreements, parent values, religious standards—all embody common values, the need to avoid engaging in actions that could hurt others or the common good.[15]

Influence of Others

Doing What They Say: Social Manipulation

Young people who are at higher risk when using digital technologies are those searching online for the love and attention they are lacking in their lives.[16] This search for love and attention is the foundation for much, if not all, online risk behavior. Social-influence techniques are used online by dangerous individuals, as well as commercial sites and advertisers that tie into this search for love and attention.[17] The most common way that these techniques are used online include the following:

- *Sending overly friendly messages.* Everyone wants attention— at-risk youth crave attention. So dangerous individuals will send overly friendly messages. They frequently use an

---

[15] This is addressed more fully in Chapter 15.

[16] Berkman Internet Safety Task Force, supra; Collier & Nigam, supra.

[17] The insight for this analysis was derived from an excellent book on these influence techniques that likely should be required reading for all high school students. Cialdini, R. B. (2008). *Influence: Science and practice* (5th ed). Needham Heights, MA: Allyn and Bacon.

operant conditioning approach of excessive compliments, and other "rewards" for the behavior, proceeding step-by-step to their end objective. This is the same technique trainers use to teach a dolphin to turn in a circle.

- *Offers of gifts or opportunities.* Sites may offer gifts in exchange for providing personal information used for advertising. Dangerous individuals may offer an opportunity such as assistance in obtaining a modeling job.
- *Encouraging a commitment to a special relationship.* Dangerous individuals often are overly eager in trying to establish a close relationship. Companies or organizations encourage people to sign up, establish a friendship link, or indicate that they "like" a product.

Follow the Leaders: Influence of Legitimate Authority

Young people are motivated to act in accordance with those whom they consider to be legitimate authorities. This includes important adults in their lives. This fact must be handled carefully, because sometimes young people may not perceive adults to fully understand their digital culture and thus may not consider them to be authorities. The influence of authority must be deemed as legitimate.

Strategies

Encourage students to be wary of anyone online who is being overly friendly and overly eager to form a relationship. Students often refer to these people as *creeps*. Students should always reflect on what they are being asked to provide in exchange for anything "free." More comprehensive strategies are necessary to address the concerns of those students who are at much higher risk.[18]

The objective of any person acting in the role of authority must be to focus attention on common values that are supported by positive social norms and less on the potential for detection and punishment. Consider who is likely to have the greatest legitimacy in the eyes of students on any issue related to the use of digital technologies. Using older students to talk with younger students is an excellent way to provide insight.

---

[18] These strategies are discussed in Chapter 4.

The Dangers of Techno-Panic

A critical issue that must be addressed is recognizing and avoiding the presentation of messages to students that are grounded in techno-panic. Unfortunately, at this time, a significant level of techno-panic has been incorporated into the curriculum and messaging that students receive.

WHAT IS TECHNO-PANIC?

Techno-panic is a heightened level of concern about use of contemporary technologies by young people that is disproportionate to the empirical data on the actual degree of risk.[1] Moral panic is when a "condition, episode, person or group of persons emerges to become defined as a threat to societal systems and interests."[2] Techno-panic appears to be a moral panic in response to fear of modernity and change as represented by new technologies.[3]

Often, purveyors of techno-panic have underlying motives. Organizations seeking funding to address Internet safety have been known to overhype the risks. Fear-based messages are often conveyed by companies seeking to sell "technology quick-fixes" to parents. Other times, the techno-panic has come from law enforcement officials who have an unfortunate tendency to focus on fear.

---

[1] Roush, W. (2006, August 7). The moral panic over social-networking sites. *Technology Review.* Retrieved June 22, 2011, from http://www.technologyreview.com/communications/17266/?a=f

[2] Cohen, S. (1972). *Folk devils and moral panics: The creation of the Mods and Rockers.* London: MacGibbon and Kee, p. 9.

[3] Marwick, A. (2008, June). To catch a predator: The MySpace moral panic. *First Monday, 13*(6). Retrieved June 22, 2011, from http://www.uic.edu/htbin/cgiwrap/bin/ojs/index.php/fm/article/view/2152/1966

The widespread fear about young people online is *not* supported by the research data.[4] Young people who are at greatest risk online appear to be those who are already at greater risk in general. Thus, this is youth risk behavior that is now manifesting with the use of these technologies. Extensive research has demonstrated that seeking to transmit fear is ineffective as a risk-prevention approach. Furthermore, the Internet safety warnings about adult "stranger danger" are not supported by the research. Young people face greater risks from known peers.

None of the following discussion is intended to convey the idea that we should not be concerned about the minority of young people who do face serious risks, are harmed, or are engaging in risky or harmful behavior. To effectively address these concerns, however, it is absolutely critical to have an accurate understanding.

EXAMPLES OF TECHNO-PANIC

One in Seven Teens Has Been Solicited Online by a Sexual Predator

For the last decade, much of the techno-panic has been related to online sexual predators. On many law enforcement websites, there are statements related to the sexual solicitation of young people, ostensibly by these online predators:

- National Center for Missing and Exploited Children website: "And there is another shocking number: 1 in 7 children are solicited online for sex. Sexual predators are exploiting the Internet to victimize children."[5]
- Florida Attorney General's website: "Nationally, one in seven children between the ages of ten and 17 have been solicited online by a sexual predator."[6]

A study did find that one in seven young people were "sexually solicited" online, but not primarily by adult sexual predators.[7] The survey, conducted by the Crimes Against Children Research Center (CACRC), asked about the receipt of "unwanted communications of a sexual nature." These messages came from other teens (43 percent) or young adults (30 percent). Only 8 percent came from older adults. The teens receiving

---

[4] Berkman Internet Safety Task Force, supra; Collier & Nigam, supra.

[5] Retrieved June 22, 2011, from http://www.take25.org/page.asp?page=86

[6] Retrieved June 22, 2011, from http://myfloridalegal.com/pages.nsf/Main /DF75DF6F54BDA68E8525727B00645478

[7] Wolak et al. (2006), supra.

messages handled them effectively. The majority (66 percent) were not upset or frightened.

In 2006, the arrests for online sexual predation involving real teen victims accounted for 1 percent of all arrests for the sexual abuse of minors, just over six hundred teens.[8] This study also found that, contrary to common Internet safety messaging, predators are not tracking and abducting youth based on personal contact information posted online and rarely engage in deception or violence. Teens meet with these adults knowing they are adults and intending to engage in sex.

Cyberbullying Is an Epidemic

Many news articles are reporting that incidents of cyberbullying are at an epidemic level. Frequently, the news reports also state that there has been a significant increase in youth suicide caused by cyberbullying. Simply type the terms *cyberbullying* and *epidemic* into a search engine and look at the results. Story upon story upon story with these two terms in the headline are evident. This is the headline statement from a press release from a company selling monitoring software: "Cyberbullying is a horrific epidemic sweeping our nation, resulting in the tragic loss of teenage life to suicide. But there is a solution."[9]

Accurate and balanced information available from Drs. Hinduja and Patchin at Cyberbullying Research Center indicates that about 20 percent of young people report they had been victim of or engaged in cyberbullying at some point in their life. The degree to which they were distressed by these incidents ranges.[10]

One in Five Teens Has Sent a Nude Sexy Photo

A common statement about sexting that appears in news stories is this: "In a 2008 study by the National Campaign to Prevent Teen and Unplanned Pregnancy, 22 percent of teenage girls who responded said they had been texted or had posed for nude or seminude photos."[11] The oft-cited statistic came from an opt-in web survey conducted by a

---

[8] Wolak, J., Finklehor, D., & Mitchel, K. (2009). Trends in arrests of "online predators." *Crimes Against Children Research Center*. Retrieved June 22, 2011, from http://www.unh.edu/ccrc/pdf/CV194.pdf

[9] Shallcross, K. (2010, November 10). Stop cyberbullying now with computer monitoring software. *PRWeb*. Retrieved June 22, 2011, from http://www.prweb.com/releases/PCPandora/StopCyber bullying/prweb4769414.htm; see also Cyber bullying: How can we keep our children from becoming victims? (2010, October 7). *SpectorSoft*. Retrieved June 22, 2011, from http://spectorsoft.blogspot .com/2010/10/cyber-bullying-how-can-we-keep-our.html

[10] Patchin, J. W., & Hinduja, S. (2011). Cyberbullying: An update and synthesis of the research. In J. W. Patchin & S. Hinduja (Eds.), *Cyberbullying prevention and response: Expert perspectives* (pp. 13–35). New York, NY: Routledge.

[11] Ward, M. (2010, November 10). Texas officials proposing "sexting" legislation. *The Dallas Morning News*. Retrieved June 22, 2011, from http://www.dallasnews.com/sharedcontent/dws/news/ texassouthwest/stories/DN-sexting_10tex.ART.State.Edition1.fcb7c6.html

public-relations marketing company for the National Campaign.[12] In the press release is this statement: "Respondents do not constitute a probability sample."[13] Translation: This study cannot be used to accurately estimate the actual occurrence among the general population.

Compare the results of this study with one conducted by the Pew Internet and American Life Project.[14] This study was of a random sample of youth age thirteen to seventeen. Pew found that just 4 percent of cell-owning teens ages twelve to seventeen said they had sent sexually suggestive nude or nearly nude photos of themselves to someone else via text messaging.

TECHNO-PANIC AND THE DAMAGING IMPACT ON WEB 2.0 IN SCHOOLS

Trying to prepare students for their future education, careers, personal lives, and civic responsibilities and teaching digital safety and civility without Web 2.0 interactive technologies in schools is like trying to teach a child how to swim without a swimming pool. In addition to being totally ineffective in preventing risk behavior, techno-panic can also present a significant barrier to adoption of Web 2.0 interactive technologies and the transformation of schools into 21st-century learning environments.[15]

An approach to understanding the factors that present barriers to technology adoption in schools is grounded in the work of Geoffery Moore.[16] According to Moore, there is a significant chasm between the early adopters of technology, whom he calls the *visionaries*, and the next adoption group, whom he calls the *pragmatists*.

The reason for this chasm is that the individuals in these two groups function in a different manner. Visionaries are intuitive thinkers, who are willing to take reasonable risks. Give visionaries a 75 percent solution, and they will "jump in and invent" the rest as things go forward. Pragmatists

---

[12] National Campaign to Prevent Teen and Unplanned Pregnancy (2008). *Sex and tech: Results from a survey of teens and young adults.* Retrieved June 22, 2011, from http://www.thenationalcampaign.org/sextech/PDF/SexTech_Summary.pdf. The name of the public relations company is TRU: http://trugroup.com/TRU-market-research.html

[13] http://www.thenationalcampaign.org/sextech/press.aspx

[14] Lenhart, A. (2009, December 15). *Teens and sexting: How and why minor teens are sending sexually suggestive nude or nearly nude images via text messaging.* Washington, DC: Pew Internet and American Life Project. Retrieved June 22, 2011, from http://www.pewinternet.org/~/media//Files/Reports/2009/PIP_Teens_and_Sexting.pdf

[15] Consider the impact of Internet safety materials *provided for schools by the North Carolina Attorney General.* According to the booklet *Internet Safety: What You Don't Know Can Hurt Your Children*, "Hazards that begin with innocent computer use can threaten the safety of students under your care." Furthermore, "A child can get into serious trouble sitting right in front of a computer screen, right under your nose." Retrieved June 22, 2011, from http://nrhs.nred.org/www/nred_nrhs/site/hosting/InternetSafety DISTRICTSITE/InternetSafetyVideos/WhatYouDontKnowCanHURTgov.pdf

[16] Moore, G. (1991). *Crossing the chasm: Marketing and selling high-tech products to mainstream customers.* New York, NY: HarperBusiness; Moore, G. (1995). *Inside the tornado: Marketing strategies from Silicon Valley's cutting edge.* New York, NY: HarperBusiness.

also want to move forward, but they are analytical and focus on managing risks. Discontinuous change—doing things in a totally new way—will only occur when a sufficient number of pragmatists have shifted to the new direction.

The width of the chasm is directly controlled by the degree of perceived risk associated with the use of digital technologies. Given that pragmatists seek to manage the risks, the misperception that these risks are significant contributes to greater reluctance to change. When we effectively address the misperceptions that are leading to significant fear of interactive technologies—through effective positive social norms–based digital safety and civility education—this will also help to provide the essential conditions necessary for schools to more effectively transition to 21st-century learning environments. Conversely, if schools use fear-based Internet safety education, or invite outside presenters who impart fear that students are at great risk online, the ability of that school to effectively transition to 21st-century instructional environments will be seriously undermined.

The Cyber Savvy approach acknowledges the actual risks, as identified by research, but seeks to address these risks by focusing on positive social norms and effective strategies. In addition to this positive messaging, conducting local Cyber Savvy surveys will provide insight from local students about the actual rates of negative incidents, as well as insight into the effectiveness of strategies used by students. This insight, which can be shared with parents and the community, should help to overcome techno-panic and to support the shift to 21st-century instruction.

EFFECTIVENESS OF CURRICULUM AND MESSAGING

The CACRC has received a grant to study the effectiveness of Internet safety programs that have received funding through the U.S. Department of Justice.[17] This should include the programs of I-Safe, NetSmartz, IKeepSafe, WebWiseKids, as well as the resources created by the state Internet Crimes Against Children task forces. Comments about this evaluation were made by Dr. Finklehor, director of the center, in the recent Online Safety and Technologies Working Group report.[18] The following is a brief summary of the comments.

- At this point in time, Internet safety education programs, including those that are promoted for use by law enforcement, have not been comprehensively evaluated to determine effectiveness.

---

[17] Jones, L. (2009, October 1). UNH Crimes Against Children Research Center receives more than $480,000 to fight Internet crimes against children. *University of New Hampshire Media Relations.* Retrieved June 22, 2011, from http://www.unh.edu/news/cj_nr/2009/oct/lw01crimes.cfm

[18] Collier & Nigam, supra, p. 25.

- Many current programs do not appear to be based on an accurate understanding of the risks and may not result in any changes in behavior.
- The delivery of instruction to address Internet safety must be incorporated into comprehensive social-emotional development instruction and provide guidance in effective problem solving and decision making.
- Research has clearly demonstrated that fear-based messages, which are evident in some of these materials, are not effective risk prevention.[19]

While this book suggests a primary reliance on locally developed, positive peer norms–based instructional opportunities, some districts may also want to acquire formal curriculum materials to use in conjunction with this approach. Fortunately, newer curriculum is becoming available. Recommended resources will be identified on the Cyber Savvy website http://embracingdigitalyouth.org.

It is essential to carefully assess both the source and quality of any curriculum materials that are adopted, as well as any outside presenters. Engage in the following assessment steps:

- Determine the organization or individual's underlying area of expertise.
- Request information on the research insight and risk-prevention approach that has been relied on in creating the curriculum or developing the presentation.
- Evaluate the curriculum to determine whether it uses any of the following problematical approaches. Ask presenters for references for past presentations and make inquiries related to these issues.

The following are approaches to avoid and alternatives to adopt:

- Avoid material or presentations that communicate the misperception that many young people are at risk online or are engaging in unsafe or irresponsible actions.
  - Choose material or presenters that communicate positive messages that the majority of young people make safe and responsible decisions and effectively respond to negative situations.
- Avoid material or presentations that impart inaccurate, fear-based information and messaging.
  - Choose material or presenters that provide insight grounded in research on actual risks and degree of harm associated with those risks.

---

[19] This summary statement was approved by Drs. Finklehor and Jones.

- Avoid material or presenters that impart simplistic rules against normative online behavior like rules against communicating with any online strangers or posting photos of oneself or of friends online.
  - Choose materials and presenters that focus on problem solving and skill building.
- Avoid material or presenters that impart "stranger danger" warnings and try to make it appear that anyone they meet online is highly likely to want to harm them.
  - Instead, choose material or presenters that focus on strategies young people can use to safely interact online with people who are known in person or not.
- Avoid instructional approaches that rely primarily on adults directly instructing secondary students. However, sometimes this approach can be useful, for example, having a law enforcement official make a special presentation.
  - Create situations where the majority of the instruction engages students in talking with their peers.
- Avoid having students sign "Internet safety pledges."
  - Encourage students to develop their own statements of personal standards.
- Avoid recommending that parents of teens strongly rely on filtering or monitoring technologies.
  - Recommend that parents place their strongest emphasis on active and positive interactions, use protective technologies for children, and constructively use monitoring technologies for tweens and at-risk teens.

CONCERNS RELATED TO "CYBERBULLYING CAUSES SUICIDE" CURRICULUM AND MESSAGING

Of significant current concern is messaging, including curriculum and presenters, that focuses on the message that cyberbullying and sexting are "causing" young people to suicide.[20] Suicide is invariably the result of multiple factors.[21] Bullying, cyberbullying, and sexual harassment can contribute to a young person's distress and, in some cases, could be a trigger for

---

[20] Bazelon. E. (2011, April 4). How not to prevent bullying: Two anti-bullying videos that might do more harm than good. *Slate*. Retrieved June 22, 2011, from http://www.slate.com/id/2282773/

[21] Centers for Disease Control and Prevention, National Institute of Mental Health, Office of the Surgeon General, Substance Abuse and Mental Health Services Administration, American Foundation for Suicide Prevention, American Association of Suicidology, et al. (n.d.). *Reporting on suicide: Recommendations for the media*. Retrieved June 22, 2011, from http://www.sprc.org/library/sreporting.pdf. This document provides guidance for news reporting that also is directly applicable to curriculum, presentations, and other messaging.

suicide—but it is never a cause.[22] Blaming individuals who engaged in bullying for a suicide can lead young people to think that if someone suicides, another person is to blame. The placement of blame and resulting guilt can significantly impair the recovery of survivors of suicide.[23]

Suicide contagion or "copy cat" suicide is the most serious concern. This nation's suicide-prevention professionals have issued clear guidance on this for news reporting that also should apply to any instruction:

> Dramatizing the impact of suicide through descriptions and pictures of grieving relatives, teachers or classmates or community expressions of grief may encourage potential victims to see suicide as a way of getting attention or as a form of retaliation against others.[24]

Schools are strongly advised to avoid selecting any curriculum or presenters who

- focus on fear that cyberbullying will cause suicide as an attempt to reduce risk behavior;
- provide inaccurate information related to bullying or cyberbullying causing suicide;
- present stories where young people suicide and tie this to bullying or cyberbullying;
- provide information on the means used by young people who have suicided
- point the finger of blame at those who engaged in hurtful behavior; or
- present teens as stereotypical mean and nasty people.

Any presentation related to suicide associated with cyberbullying should only be conveyed by someone with significant expertise in suicide prevention. It is exceptionally important to present to teens messages of hope and resilience and to provide guidance on suicide prevention and what to do if they witness someone who is in distress.

---

[22] Suicide Prevention Resource Center. (2011, March). *Suicide and bullying: Issue brief.* Retrieved June 15, 2011, from http://www.sprc.org/library/Suicide_Bullying_Issue_Brief.pdf

[23] Jackson. J. (2003). SOS: *A handbook for survivors of suicide.* Washington, DC: American Association of Suicidology. Retrieved June 22, 2011, from http://library.sprc.org/getitem.php?id=170&res=url

[24] Centers for Disease Control and Prevention et al., supra.

Youth at High Risk Online

Prevention and Intervention

The digital safety and civility education that is the focus of *Cyber Savvy* will provide the foundation for more comprehensive risk prevention and intervention programs in the school. This chapter will briefly set forth insight related to the targeted risk-prevention and -intervention initiatives that are also necessary to address the concerns presented by the minority of young people who are at higher risk.[1] These higher risk concerns include the following:

- Digital aggression
- Risky sexual and relationship issues
- Unsafe or dangerous groups
- Underlying concerns related to unsafe postings, unsafe interactions with others, and addictive access

As has already been noted, research has demonstrated that the young people who are at greater risk online are generally those who are at greater risk offline.[2] These at-risk young people are likely to also

- have significant psychosocial concerns, including depression, social anxiety, anger responses, and suicidal ideation;
- engage in other risk-taking behavior and aggression;
- have friends who are also at risk and engage in risk behavior; and
- have poor relations with parents or other caregivers.

---

[1] The author has also written *Cyberbullying and Cyberthreats: Responding to the Challenge of Online Social Aggression and Threats* (2007), published by Research Press.

[2] Berkman Internet Safety Technical Task Force, supra; Collier & Nigam, supra.

This risk behavior when using digital technologies is generally grounded in mental health concerns, or the concern that victimization could lead to mental health concerns. Because many incidents involve known peers, such behavior will often cause a disruptive or harmful impact at school. At the more egregious level, this risk behavior could result in criminal victimization or a violation of criminal law.[3]

It appears that the higher the degree of risk, the greater the probability a teen will be

- more vulnerable to manipulation;
- emotionally upset, and thus less likely to make good choices because he or she is not thinking clearly, resulting in hurtful or damaging materials distributed in digital format;
- less attentive to Internet safety messages delivered by adults;
- less resilient in getting out of a difficult situation, even if the teen wants to;
- less able or willing to rely on parents or other adults for assistance;
- more likely to be associating with other youth in real life or online who are also engaged in risk behavior; and
- less likely to report an online dangerous situation to an adult, because this will likely reveal evidence of the teen's own unsafe or inappropriate choices.

TRIANGLE MODEL AND THE ROLE OF PEERS

The "triangle" model that is applied in health-related prevention focuses on primary, secondary, and tertiary prevention and intervention.

Primary or *universal prevention* includes imparting the basic skills, knowledge, and behavioral information that all young people require to support their safe and responsible use of digital technologies. All students require this understanding.

Secondary prevention applies to the young people who are at higher risk and involves imparting more sophisticated insight to these young people. The issues, related to digital aggression and sexual and relationship concerns, are more focused on secondary prevention. It is highly recommended that instruction be delivered by counselors and health teachers, who generally address these higher risk subjects. Counselors and school resource officers may also provide additionally personal counseling.

---

[3]This is discussed in Chapters 5 and 15.

Tertiary intervention addresses those high-risk youth who are engaging in risk behavior, have been harmed, or are harming others.

It is essential that increased focus be placed on the role of peers within the framework of this risk-prevention triangle, as the importance of the role of peers related to use of digital technologies has been consistently underscored in the research literature:

- *The EU Kids Online survey.*[4] In every risk area—digital aggression, unwanted sexual contact, and meeting in person with someone they had gotten to know online—the young people were more inclined to discuss these situations with friends.
- *Crimes Against Children Research Center.*[5] After receiving unwanted sexual or hurtful communications, young people were more likely to tell a friend or sibling than a parent or other adult.
- *The Youth Voice Project.*[6] Students were more likely to report traditional bullying incidents to friends than to school officials. Furthermore, the situations more often worsened after reporting to a school official than when they reported to friends.

To infuse the role of peers into the risk-prevention triangle, consider the ways in which peer influence or actions can assist in preventing risk behavior or responding to negative situations:

- *Primary.* When young people clearly understand the positive social norms held by a majority of their peers, negative behavior decreases. If students learn the effective practices and strategies used by their peers, they are more likely to implement these same practices and strategies. Communicate these positive peer norms, practices, and strategies.
- *Secondary.* Because young people who are involved in a negative situation are more likely to reach out for assistance from a friend, help students gain the necessary skills to assist their friends in responding to negative situations.
- *Tertiary.* Young people will witness negative digital situations more frequently than adults. Ensure that young people can recognize the more serious concerns, know how to raise their concerns

---

[4] Livingstone et al., supra.

[5] Wolak et al. (2006), supra.

[6] Davis, S., & Nixon, C. (2010, March). *Preliminary results from the Youth Voice Research Project: Victimization and strategies.* Youth Voice Project. Retrieved June 22, 2011, from http://www.youthvoiceproject.com/YVPMarch2010.pdf

to their friends, and know the importance of reporting serious or unresolved situations to a responsible adult.

TARGETED RISK PREVENTION AND INTERVENTION

Effective targeted risk prevention and intervention will require a collaborative, multidisciplinary approach involving all participants in safe school planning—administrators, counselors/psychologists, health teachers, and school resource officers. It is very important that educational technology specialists be added to this group. These comprehensive activities are beyond the scope of this book. Components of a comprehensive approach include the following:

- Multidisciplinary collaboration
- Needs assessment
- Evaluation and modification school plans and policies
- Professional development
- Parent and community outreach
- Student education
- Evaluation

ONLINE INFORMATION AND SUPPORT SERVICES

There are excellent online information and support services directed at youth who are facing questions and concerns, including those at higher risk. The online environment itself can be used to provide information, self-help resources, individual or network-based support, and crisis intervention.[7] The ability to seek help "invisibly" online may support greater help-seeking behavior by those who are at risk or by their friends who are seeking information to provide assistance.

There are many excellent examples of organizations that are using social media to provide youth risk-prevention information and support programs. These include Suicide Prevention Lifeline, The Trevor Project, To Write Love on Her Arms, A Thin Line, and It Gets Better.[8]

Instruction related to finding accurate and helpful health and well-being information online is advised. This instruction will provide the

---

[7] Centers for Disease Control and Prevention. (2010). *The health communicator's social media toolkit.* Retrieved June 22, 2011, from http://www.cdc.gov/healthcommunication/ToolsTemplates/SocialMediaToolkit_BM.pdf

[8] http://www.suicidepreventionlifeline.org/; http://www.thetrevorproject.org/; http://www.twloha.com/; http://www.athinline.org/; http://www.itgetsbetter.org/

opportunity to introduce these support sites. A school could also set up a webpage that would link directly to these kinds of sites.

ENSURING A LIKELIHOOD OF SUCCESS

Risk-prevention professionals place a high degree of reliance on programs that have demonstrated, through comprehensive research, that they are effective. The challenge in addressing the risk behaviors involving digital technologies is complicated by the fact that there is insufficient research on these concerns and that the technology field keeps changing.

The objective of using evidence-based best practice is to ensure a likelihood of success. Thus, without the benefit of evidence-based best practices, it is necessary to focus on other strategies to ensure success.[9] The key strategies that have been relied on in the writing of *Cyber Savvy:*

- *Ground prevention and intervention in an understanding of the current research.* As will become evident in Part II, the guidance in *Cyber Savvy* is grounded in research insight.
- *Adapt approaches that have been demonstrated effective to address other risk behavior to meet these new concerns.* The Cyber Savvy positive social norms prevention approach has demonstrated effectiveness in preventing risk behavior.
- *Conduct needs assessment and regularly evaluate the effectiveness of the program.* The Cyber Savvy approach encourages districts to conduct local surveys for needs assessment and evaluation. Thus, the Cyber Savvy surveys are a vitally important component of the overall strategy to ensure effectiveness.

---

[9] These recommendations are based on guidelines provided by the Office of Safe and Drug Free Schools to achieve a waiver of the requirement that funded programs meet the standard of principles of effectiveness. Title IV, Part A. Section 4115(a)(3). Retrieved June 22, 2011, from http://www2.ed.gov/legislation/ESEA02/pg52.html

Law Enforcement Officers as Instructors

The most important reason for the involvement of law enforcement officers is that the more significant youth risk online concerns can cross over into the criminal dimension—the young person may be either criminally victimized or at risk of such victimization or may engage in criminal action.[1]

Recalling the discussion of the need to understand the whole elephant, unfortunately, law enforcement officials get to be stationed at the rear end of this beast. So their perspectives can be shaped by the "excrement" they see and learn of through law enforcement channels. It is exceptionally important that law officers see the whole elephant and understand that only a minority of young people are at serious risk.

The very important lessons that have been learned by the Drug Abuse Resistance Education (DARE) program must inform efforts related to law officers providing instruction related to digital safety and civility.[2] When DARE started, there were legitimate concerns about drug abuse and violence among youth. Although the DARE program was popular, it was found through countless studies to be totally ineffective.[3] This was the conclusion of the congressional General Accounting Office (GAO), the U.S. Surgeon General, the National Academy of Sciences, and the U.S. Department of Education.

---

[1] These issues are also addressed in Chapter 15.

[2] http://www.dare.org

[3] Hansen, D. J. (n.d.). Drug Abuse Resistance Education: The effectiveness of DARE. *Alcoholfacts.org*. Retrieved June 22, 2011, from http://www.alcoholfacts.org/DARE.html

During the last decade, DARE implemented a program under conditions that included longitudinal evaluation. Unfortunately, this program was also found to be ineffective.[4] As a result of this finding, DARE has shifted to a new program that is focused on positive social norms and effective skills: "keepin' it REAL."[5] Essentially, the insight gained by DARE to avoid fear and authoritarian delivery, and instead to focus on positive norms and effective skills, must be applied to address these concerns about digital safety and civility.

Much of the funding for the preparation of Internet safety materials that are currently available has come through the U.S. Department of Justice. The approach taken in these resources resembles early-stage DARE, except that sometimes the information conveyed is not even accurate. As noted in Chapter 3, these materials are currently being evaluated by the Crimes Against Children Research Center. Concerns have already been noted about the accuracy and effectiveness of these materials. These materials were developed prior to more recent research evidence that has better outlined the concerns, and the materials do not incorporate approaches that are recognized as effective in preventing risk behavior.

It is presumed that law enforcement officials' involvement will likely be limited to one-time events—either an assembly or an appearance in a classroom—or other more short-term instructional opportunities. This also presents a concern because it is well known that such limited presentations do not generally have a high level of effectiveness. Furthermore, while law officers understand things such as arresting a suspect or conducting a search, they are not trained educators.

These law enforcement–guided instructional opportunities should cover important information about when lines are crossed related to criminal actions. This is necessary insight for students. This insight can then be reinforced by the teachers.

TOPICS TO ADDRESS

The important issues that a law enforcement official should address with students include the following:

- All aspects related to youth sexual exploitation, including the possibility of meeting someone online who might intend to exploit

---

[4] Newest DARE program, "Take Charge of Your Life," is ineffective and counterproductive. (n.d.). *Alcohol Problems and Solutions*. Retrieved June 22, 2011, from http://www2.potsdam.edu/hansondj/YouthIssues/20091103204034.html

[5] http://www.dare.com/newdare.asp

them sexually by seeking nude photos or a sexual encounter, sexting, and digital dating abuse.

- Accessing or distributing child pornography. Students must be informed about the potential of criminal prosecution for this, as well as the strategies law enforcement is using to detect these activities. It is essential to make sure that students do not think they are invisible when using peer-to-peer networking or other online venues to obtain this kind of material.
- Incidents where hurtful digital behavior can be considered a criminal violation, including laws related to cyberstalking, cyber-harassment, invasion of privacy, hate crimes, and the like.
- Online threats, including threats of violence or suicide.
- Unsafe online communities that can lead a young person to engagement in illegal activities, such as drug abuse, hate crimes, trafficking in child pornography, or sexual trafficking of minors.

REACHING THE POTENTIAL HELPFUL ALLIES

Consider the primary target for these limited instructional opportunities. All students must know when these risk situations have "crossed the line" and involve criminal matters—either as victimization or violation—and know how to prevent themselves and friends from getting into risky situations, detect when they are, and respond. However, it is unlikely that a visiting officer will be very effective in reaching those students who are at higher risk. We know these at-risk students do not generally trust adults. Absent a healthy ongoing relationship, these students are the ones who can be predicted to be least likely to listen to what a law officer might have to say about risks.

Therefore, the primary target for law officer presentations should be those students who already have a higher degree of trust in adults, that is, the students who are not at high risk but who are very likely to be present in digital environments where the higher risk students are at risk or harming others. These presentations provide the opportunity to ensure these savvier students understand the serious concerns, recognize how harmful the consequences might be, and know how important it is to try to warn their peers and to report serious concerns to school leadership or the police.

The next very important question is, what could prevent these savvier youth from listening to a law officer? Answer: if they are told they also are at high risk. These savvier youth are far less likely to be at risk because they are far more likely to be making good choices and to effectively detect and respond if a negative or risk situation emerges. If a law officer tries to convince these savvier youth they are at risk when using digital technologies, it is highly likely they will simply "tune out."

The following are recommendations for how an officer can frame a presentation that will have a higher likelihood of reaching the broadest number of students, especially those who will be most likely to effectively detect and report serious concerns.

- Introduce the topic of online risks. Immediately acknowledge that you know that the majority of young people make good choices online and are generally able to resolve the negative situations that do occur. If the school has done the surveying that is recommended, recognize and acknowledge that this is what their own data has already demonstrated.
- Indicate that you are here to talk about the more serious risks that are faced by only a minority of young people and that these risk include situations where they may be harmed by others or may themselves engage in conduct that is a violation of the law.
  - You might ask the students how many of them have seen situations where someone they know has made a bad choice— when someone is hurting someone else or is doing something online that could lead to their being harmed. It is likely that hands will be raised.
- Indicate that your job as a law officer is to make sure that young people are not being harmed, but that this job is difficult when teens are interacting with others in digital environments because you are not generally hanging out in these environments—nor do you expect that they would want you to.
- Indicate that the primary reason for your presentation is not to try to make them think they are at risk, but the plain fact is that they are more likely to see when others are at risk. If they know what the more serious risks are, they will be able to tell a friend that he or she is doing something that could end up causing harm—to their friend or someone else. Furthermore, if they see that someone is being harmed or at risk of being harmed and they report this to a principal, counselor, or school officer, or even call the police, they could play a very important role in preventing this harm from occurring or getting worse.
- From here, the discussion should address the higher risks outlined previously and addressed more fully in Chapters 16, 19, and 20. As you interact with students, you can ask important questions:
  - What are the key things people need to do to avoid getting into this kind of a situation?
  - How can you detect if you or a friend might be at risk?

    o What steps can you take or advise your friend to take to get out of a risky situation?

    o When should you report possible concerns to a responsible adult?

PRESENTATIONS FOR PARENTS

A problem law enforcement officers face when talking to parents is that the parents of the children who are most likely to be at risk are generally not the parents who will attend a presentation on Internet safety presented by a law officer. Therefore, the objective of these presentations should also be focused on imparting information about the higher risks and encouraging these attentive parents to communicate to their likely savvier children the need to pay attention to when someone might be at risk and the know-how to provide guidance, as well as the importance of reporting serious concerns.[6]

EVALUATIONS

As noted in Chapter 4, a commitment to the assessment of effectiveness is very important. This is especially important with presentations that are more limited in scope and time. A specific law enforcement instruction evaluation survey will be provided on the Cyber Savvy website, http://embracingdigitalyouth.org. This will address insight gained and the likelihood that the presentation has changed behavior, especially the degree to which students appear to recognize the importance of reporting serious concerns.

---

[6] More guidance on presenting to parents is provided in Chapter 7.

School Staff Online

This chapter addresses an additional area of education that the digital safety and civility team likely should address. School staff across this country are being fired, and some even arrested, because of actions taken when using digital technologies in interactions with students. The following information is important to communicate to all school staff.

IN PUBLIC ONLINE—ALWAYS

School staff members have an important job that relates directly to the safety and well-being of the young people who have been entrusted to their care. Thus, what they post online—or what others post about them—can provide the basis for disciplinary consequences.

School staff must take the perspective they will always be "in public" on the Internet. Everything a school staff member does online, including information and photos posted, as well as the friends they link to, could be used to judge their character. Furthermore, anything that a school staff member sends in a digital format could easily become very public.

Concerns also relate to what friends of school staff might post that discloses unflattering information about the staff member, especially tagged pictures. Staff should never place themselves in a position where a photo could be captured of them that could be embarrassing. In some regions of the country, this could include photos of them drinking at an adult party.

DISCIPLINARY ISSUES

Issues related to discipline of school staff vary by state. This information is more general in nature. Probationary staff are employed "at will," and thus school officials have flexibility in imposing discipline. Tenured staff can only be removed for "cause," which is generally unprofessional or immoral conduct—frequently defined by statute. If such conduct is determined to exist, there must be an assessment of whether this is remediable or irremediable. Irremediable conduct is conduct that has caused significant damage or that the staff member refuses to change. Evidence of criminal conduct may be considered irremediable. If not clearly irremediable, school officials must assess the nexus of the conduct to the staff member's performance and whether the conduct has significantly and negatively affected the staff member's ability to do his or her job. All material will be used to ask one question: "Is this staff member the kind of person we trust to be responsible for our children?"

A public school district's right to discipline is limited by the First Amendment, which protects a staff member's right to speak as a citizen about matters of public concern under most circumstances.[1] A staff member may establish that his or her speech is constitutionally protected if the staff member's interest as a citizen in commenting on matters of public concern outweighs the interest of the district.

The Federal Educational Rights and Privacy Act provides protections for student privacy, with very stringent consequences if school staff violate these protections.[2] Staff must know that it is never permissible to discuss students through materials posted or sent in digital format, except as specifically governed through district communication channels.

USE OF SOCIAL NETWORKING SITES

School staff who want to use social networking sites, such as Facebook, for personal activities should use privacy protections to generally limit access to their personal information, but they should recognize that these protections will not prevent public disclosure. Thus, even with these protections, a school staff member should take the perspective that anything posted or sent in digital format could be on the front page of tomorrow's newspaper. The more embarrassing or damaging the material a school staff member posts online or sends digitally, the more likely it will end up being brought to the attention of a school administrator.

---

[1] Connick v. Myers, 461 U.S. 138 (1983).

[2] 20 U.S.C. § 1232g.

School staff also must be scrupulously careful whenever communicating with strangers, that is, someone not know in person. This includes establishing a friendship with a stranger on their social networking profile. Creative students have been very effective in tricking school staff into believing that a fake profile is the man or woman of their dreams and then shared the staff member's personal communications and photos.

SOCIALIZING WITH STUDENTS

School staff should avoid engaging in online socializing with students, especially on social networking sites. *Socializing* means mixing socially, being friends. There are important distinctions in status. Just as we encourage parents to strive to be parents, not their child's friend, teachers can be positive, friendly mentors but should not engage with students in "friendship" environments. This concern does not include friendly communications related to assignments or school activities that are limited to district email or a district Web 2.0 instructional environment.

Sometimes extracurricular organizations may set up a social networking presence. Staff involvement in these arenas that are focused on the activities of the organization should be safe; but staff should make sure that they use features that will limit access to their more personal profile and interactions.

The concerns of staff–student online socializing include the following:

- *People flirt in online socializing environments.* If a student sends a flirtatious message to a staff member and he or she responds warmly, this could lead to an accusation that the staff member was involved in sexual solicitation. If the staff member responds in a disapproving manner, there is possibility of revenge. Sometimes, school staff have pursued sexual relations with students that were furthered through online socializing.[3] Sometimes, students may be the ones who are pursuing the staff. In either case, the staff member will be at high risk of ending up in serious trouble.
- *Students may send friendship requests to friends of friends.* This could then include all adult friends of the staff member. If students do not change what are the current default privacy settings on Facebook, all of a staff member's adult friends will be able to see much of the profile material of the students. The staff member could be considered a "guarantor" of all adult friends.

---

[3] Conduct a search on the terms *teacher* and *sexting* for ample evidence of this concern.

- If a teacher friends some students, but not other students, this could create a perception that these friended students are favored and, because of this, will receive better grades.
- School staff members have a legal responsibility to report suspected abuse of students and other possible harms. A staff member who has friended students and fails to detect a posting that raises concerns of abuse could face accusations that he or she violated standards for mandatory reporting.
- There are student privacy issues to be mindful of. No student should be compelled to provide access to a protected profile or establish a friendship link with a school staff member as a condition of participating in a school activity.
- Online communications between staff members and students have a significant potential of leading to a violation of the Federal Education Rights and Privacy Act by the staff member.

There are very helpful ways that schools can use social network pages for public outreach, such as a page for the school or the school library, or a page or a group for an extracurricular organization. Pages should be created by a school or a department, not an individual staff member. All use of the page or group features should be approved by school administration. Specific guidelines must be established for what kinds of material will be placed on a district-affiliated page or a school-affiliated group.

For interactive instructional activities, the use of public social networking sites is strongly discouraged. These are social environments, not instructional environments. There are many high quality social networking–like environments that are specifically designed for instructional activities. However, teachers must be able to easily bypass the district filter to allow students to access instructionally related resources that are on these sites.

Districts should ensure there is a policy that addresses inappropriate digital communications between staff and students that will allow the use of these digital technologies for appropriate instructional and school-related communications, and prevent digital socializing.

It is important that districts provide professional development for staff about responsible use of social media when outside of the school environment. Here are some guidelines:

- Never post or send material in digital format that will raise questions about character and values. Don't allow others to post such material about you.

- Use privacy protections when social networking to limit access to accepted friends, but do not think privacy protections will prevent further disclosure.
- Never friend someone you do not know in person. "Enterprising" students have effectively used fake profiles to obtain damaging information and communications.
- Use district-approved communication channels to communicate digitally with students and keep communications professional.

Recommended policy provisions for districts include:

- All school related activities, including instruction and extracurricular student organizations activities, must take place only on district-approved Web 2.0 environments.
- Staff activities on non–district-approved Internet environments, including social networking sites, should follow the following guidelines:
  - Staff must not initiate or accept friend requests from students currently enrolled in the district.
  - Staff may accept friend requests from former students who have graduated or parents but should be mindful of potential complications and should avoid discussing any school-related issues.
  - Staff may accept friend requests from other staff but should avoid discussing any school-related issues.
  - Staff should exercise extreme care in posting any information online, recognizing that this information may not remain private and could adversely impact the staff member and other members of the school community.
  - Absolutely no personal information or images of any other member of the school community or student may be posted without written permission from that person, or, in the case of a student, from the student's parent.

Schools must rapidly embrace the capabilities for instruction provided by Web 2.0 technologies, but in a manner that protects student privacy and ensures the delivery of the highest quality instruction.

Providing Parent Guidance

Schools are an important conduit of digital safety and civility education for parents. An excellent resource for schools is an online guide titled Net Cetera, which has been produced by the Federal Trade Commission.[1] This also comes with an excellent PowerPoint slide show that can be used for parent workshops. Additionally, the ConnectSafely and Common Sense Media websites contain up-to-date guidance for parents.[2]

Schools might want to consider engaging parents in the same kinds of social-norming activities as students by asking parents to complete an online survey about parenting practices. If parents find out that 70 percent of parents of middle school students have reviewed their children's privacy settings on a social networking site to make sure that their profile has been set to "friends only," this might influence the remaining 30 percent. The Cyber Savvy website at http://embracingdigitalyouth.org provides a template survey for parents.

RESEARCH INSIGHT

Several research studies are helpful in understanding the issue of effective digital parenting. These studies ground their analysis of the impact of parenting styles on Dr. Baumrind's seminal work on parenting styles.[3] Baumrind's research has found four basic styles of parenting:

---

[1] http://www.onguardonline.gov/topics/net-cetera.aspx

[2] http://www.connectsafely.org/ and http://www.commonsensemedia.org

[3] Baumrind, D. (1991). The influence of parenting style on adolescent competence and substance use. *Journal of Early Adolescence, 11*, 56–95.

1. Authoritative: actively involved in a positive manner
2. Authoritarian: actively involved but in a negative manner
3. Indulgent: positively involved but not active
4. Neglectful: negatively involved and not active

Research by Dr. Rosen and colleagues examined the relationship between parenting styles and online teen behaviors.[4] They found that the children of parents who adopted an authoritative parenting approach—where rules and limits are set but in a way that promotes warmth and caring and garners input from the teen—had fewer online risk behaviors such as personal disclosure, communicating with strangers online, and the like. Compared to teens whose parents adopted an authoritarian, indulgent, or neglectful parenting style, the children of authoritative parents were more careful online as well as being more psychologically healthy, and thus better prepared to handle any online challenges.

Drs. Hay and Meldrum conducted a study on bullying and cyberbullying, investigating such issues as suicide ideation and parenting styles.[5] This study revealed that both bullying and cyberbullying can lead to suicide ideation in some youth. However, those teens who had parents who used an authoritative parenting style that was positive and active, providing warm emotional support along with clear limits, were less emotionally distressed.

PARENTING EDUCATION OPPORTUNITIES

There are a number of formal or informal ways that schools can reach parents with important information.

Parent Workshops

Unfortunately, the parents who are likely most in need of the insight and information frequently are the parents who are least likely to attend these workshops. However, the engaged parents who will pay attention also are most likely to have children who can be important peer leaders. Focus attention on how these parents can encourage their children to assist others or report online concerns.

---

[4] Rosen, L. D., Cheever, N. A., & Carrier, L. M. (2008). The association of parenting style and child age with parental limit setting and adolescent MySpace behavior. *Journal of Applied Developmental Psychology, 29*, 459–471. Retrieved June 22, 2011, from http://www.csudh.edu/psych/The_Association_of_Parenting_Style_and_Child_Age_with_Parental_Limit_Setting_and_Adolescent_MySpace_Behavior_Journal_of_Applied_Developomental_Psychology_2008.pdf

[5] Hay, C., & Meldrum, R. (2010). Bullying, victimization and adolescent self-harm: Testing hypotheses from general strain theory. *Journal of Youth and Adolescence, 39*(5), 446–459. See also Baird, A. (2010, August 24). Best defenses against cyber bullies. *Scientific American*. Retrieved June 22, 2011, from http://www.scientificamerican.com/article.cfm?id=best-defenses-cyber-bullies/

In these workshops, it will be helpful to involve a panel of older students presenting information and their recommendations. The students could report on the results of student surveying and demonstrate the positive behaviors exhibited by their peers.

Information Resources Available at School

Schools may also provide resources in the office and library. This could include books that parents could check out, as well as the NetCetera guide. Resources can also be provided to parents in the context of parent–teacher conferences or other situations where parents come to school.

Informal Educational Opportunities

Schools can also publish brief tips in school newsletters and on district/school websites. Older students could also assist in producing these. These should provide brief positive, norms-based insight.

Outreach Tied to Instruction

It is possible for teachers to specifically tie parent education with student instruction. This is the "Mom you have to read and sign my assignment" form of parent outreach. This may also be an approach to get a select group of parents to complete a survey.

POSITIVE COMMENT

The most important strategy to recommend to parents is reliance on this specific technique: Every time they interact with their children in relation to using the digital technologies, they should be mindful of the need to make one positive statement about their children's activities. Just one positive statement per interaction—more if they are so inclined.

This is classic operant conditioning. From the child's perspective, interactions with a parent related to use of digital technologies will "feel good." Thus, the child will be more inclined to want to share aspects of his or her digital life with a parent.

FILTERING AND MONITORING TECHNOLOGIES

There are some very excellent family safety features that are provided through computer operating systems and browsers, or provided as a software or service by companies.[6] These features are also provided on

---

[6] Symantec's Norton Online Family: http://us.norton.com/familyresources/resources.jsp?title=ar_try _our_norton_online_family_service; Microsoft's Vista Family Safety technology: http://www.microsoft .com/uk/protect/products/family/vista.mspx

interactive gaming consoles. These family safety features allow parents to limit their child's access to selected sites, control who can communicate privately, manage time spent online, and review the history file. Their child should know that everything he or she does online is open to their review. These safety features can be useful in creating a "fenced play yard" for children.

Parents of tweens and teens should never expect to be able to keep their children in electronically fenced play yards using filtering software. To show parents the futility of this, simply conduct, or suggest that they conduct, a search on the term "bypass Internet filter."

The current new marketing push is for parents to install monitoring software.[7] These companies are, as is to be expected, marketing their products in a manner that communicates significant fear. Installing monitoring might be an appropriate parental response if a child appears to be at higher risk or as a logical consequence of situations where their child has engaged in wrongdoing. However, there are some significant concerns regarding reliance on monitoring technologies.

- Some preteens and early teens might be willing to accept this level of parent involvement, but a significant number of them will view this degree of intrusiveness as an indication that their parents do not trust them. This could have a negative impact on the quality of the parent–child relationship.
- Monitoring technologies can encourage passive reliance on a technology quick fix. One company actually indicates that it will review the child's friends to make sure they are safe. Isn't that a parent's job? Thus, parent involvement may become passive.

Of significant concern with some companies—those that provide monitoring for free—is that the operating model for companies involves market profiling of children's personal communications. Thus, these companies appear to be using fear as a way to obtain greater profiling and advertising access to children.[8]

GENERAL GUIDANCE FOR PARENTS

The following guidelines are appropriate for parents of children, tweens, and teens:

- *Appreciate your child's online activities.* Show interest in your child's online friends. Help your child learn to make positive choices in accord with your family's values, and comment positively every

---

[7] See information related to cyberbullying fear in Chapter 3.

[8] For example, Safe Communications: http://www.safecom.net/

time you notice that they have done something that reflects these positive values.

- *Never overreact if your child reports an online concern.* You want your child to feel comfortable reporting online concerns. Your first comment when your child reports a negative situation should be positive: "I am so glad you felt comfortable reporting this to me." Your next comment must indicate a commitment to a partnership in respond to the situation: "Can you tell me more so we can work together to figure out what to do?"

- *Use logical consequences.* If your child engages in any risky, inappropriate, or harmful behavior, impose a logical consequence that will focus your child's attention on why this action has caused or could cause harm to him or her or to someone else. Require that your child remedy any harm.

- *Pay attention to possible red flags.* Red flags include appearing emotionally upset during or after use, disturbed relationships with family members or friends, spending too much time online, engaging in excessively secretive behavior when using digital technologies, and making subtle comments about online concerns. If any red flags are evident, pay closer attention and carefully try to engage your child in discussion.

- *Encourage personal responsibility.* Encourage your child to help others directly or to report to you or another responsible adult if he or she witnesses someone being harmed or at risk online.

- *Maintain computer security.* Make sure you have implemented appropriate security against malware, use a spam blocker, block pop-up ads, and use safe search features. Never allow peer-to-peer (P2P) software, as this can lead to accidental access of pornography and is a significant source of malware that can result in identify theft.

- *Educate yourself on issues of profiling and advertising.*[9] Read the privacy policies. Pay attention to the strategies sites use to obtain your child's demographic and interest information and the various ways in which sites advertise, including targeted banner ads, ads integrated into games, and sites that ask their child to sign up to receive ads or send ads to their friends. When you recognize these profiling or advertising techniques, point them out to your child to increase his or her understanding. Take advantage of the emerging ability to restrict the ability of sites to track use for profiling.

---

[9] The best resource for insight on these issues is Common Sense Media's site, which focuses on privacy concerns: http://www.commonsensemedia.org/privacy

GUIDANCE FOR PARENTS OF CHILDREN AND TWEENS

To protect younger children, we must educate parents. When children are young, it is the parents' responsibility to make sure their Internet use is in a safe online environment and that they engage in safe communications. Children who still believe in the tooth fairy cannot be expected to protect themselves online. To them, the Internet is more of a "magic box." By third grade, young people can begin to grasp essential concepts about how the Internet functions, which provides the ability for them to take on more personal responsibility for good decision making. By middle school, many tweens will want to jump into environments and activities with teens. This shift needs to be made carefully, based in part, on an understanding of the child's social-emotional maturity.

These are strategies educators can advise parents to take for children and tweens:

- Create a "fenced play yard" for your younger child online. Limit your child's access to sites you have selected as appropriate. As your child grows, make decisions together about additional sites that are appropriate.
- Make sure you personally know everyone your child is able to communicate with through e-mail, instant messaging (IM), and any other form of personal communications. Limit communication with strangers to general areas of safe, moderated children's sites.
- Keep your family computer in a public place in your house so you can remain engaged in what your child is doing.
- If you provide a cell phone to your child or tween, implement the safety and security features provided by the company.
- If you want to allow your child to participate in a social networking environment, select a safe site that is designed for children and tweens, not teens.
- It is best not to allow your child to register on social networking sites for users over the age of thirteen. If you do allow this, go through all privacy settings to make sure that only accepted friends can see your child's profile. Have your child's login password. Insist that your child only establish friendship links with people whom he or she knows and trusts, and review all friends to make sure this is the case. Advise your child that you will regularly review his or her profile, and if any material is posted that is not safe or not in accord with your family's values, you will place restrictions on his or her use.
- Help your child create a safe and fun username that does not disclose personal details, as well as a safe password. Make sure your

child knows to never disclose his or her password to anyone other than you. Use your e-mail address for any site registrations.

SAVVY PARENTS OF TEENS

Parenting Tips

Encourage parents to be actively and positively involved with their tweens and teens by transmitting the following insights.

- Implement the use of cell phone safety and security features, if you have any concerns about your child's responsible use. Otherwise, discuss these issues of responsible use, including texting and creation of potentially damaging images of self or others. Make sure that your child turns off his or her cell phone when going to bed. If there are any problems associated with this, make sure his or her cell phone remains outside of the bedroom at night.

- When your child sets up a social networking profile, jointly go through all privacy settings to make sure that only accepted friends can see this profile. Insist initially that your child only establish friendship links with people he or she knows face-to-face and trusts. But as your child gains experience, allow the establishment of friendship links with people whom your child's friends know face-to-face and people they meet online through safe online activities. Jointly review the profile of any person whom your child does not know face-to-face to evaluate this person's values, standards, and choice of friends. Either have your child's login password (best approach when they are starting) or create your own profile and friend your child, so that you can regularly review what is happening on your child's profile, including materials posted and friends added. Advise your child that you will regularly review his or her profile, and if any material is posted that is not safe or not in accord with your family's values, you will place restrictions on his or her use.

- Keep your computer in a public area until your child is older and has demonstrated that he or she is making positive choices.

- Pay attention to what your child is doing online, but balance your supervision with your child's emerging legitimate interests in personal privacy. Positive interactions will encourage your child to share. Remember, at this age, if your child feels that you are overly intrusive, he or she could easily find a way to go behind your back. In a few short years, your child will be out of your home. It is necessary for him or her to independently make safe and responsible decisions, which requires practice in doing so.

Part II

Digital Safety and Civility Education

Cyber Safe Kids 8

SIMPLE GUIDELINES

As was stated earlier, this book is focused primarily on those students in intermediate grades up—essentially for those students who are post–tooth fairy age and are able to engage in more effective problem solving related to the issues of safe and responsible online practices.

The following instructional objectives and safely guidelines represent the kinds of simple steps that younger children can take to keep themselves safe in this environment. These objectives and guidelines correspond to chapters in Part II of this book. They provide the insight necessary to the safety of younger users and the foundation for gaining necessary skills as they grow.

INSTRUCTIONAL OBJECTIVES

Avoid the Impulse: Remember, What You Do Reflects on You

- (Grades K–3) Students will recognize that there are many websites that have material that is not designed for children and will collaborate with their parents in remaining on the sites that are safe, fun, and appropriate.

(Continued)

(Continued)

Keep Your Life in Balance: Avoid Addictive Access

- (Grades 2–3) Students will recognize that time spent using digital devices should be kept in balance with other activities.

Think Before You Post: Protect Your Personal Information and Reputation

- (Grades 2–3) Students will recognize that material posted in digital form can be provided to others and that others will judge them based on what they have posted. They will enunciate personal standards that they will only post material that will make people think they make good choices and would want to be friends with them.
- (Grades K–1) Students will recognize that they should not type their name, address, or phone number online. (Grades 2–3) Students will describe important actions to protect their personal information online, including not typing their name, address, phone number, sending a picture, or completing an online form without checking with a parent and not providing their password to anyone other than a parent.

Connect Safely: Interact Safely With Others Online (Incorporated Embrace Civility)

- (Grades K–3) Students will distinguish between personal communications, including e-mail and IM, and public sites, such as fun game sites, and will know that they should only communicate with friends through personal communications.
- (Grades K–3) Students will recognize that people can be hurtful online; indicate that if they receive a hurtful message on a public site or through a private message, they should tell an adult; and express personal standards for how they will treat others online.

Stay Out of the Garbage: Avoid "Yucky Stuff" Online

- (Grades K–3) Students will recognize that sometimes, through no fault of their own, "yucky" material could appear, and that if this happens, they should immediately turn off the screen and tell an adult. They will demonstrate the ability to rapidly turn off any computer they use while at school.

Don't Sell Yourself: Be a Wise Consumer

- (Grades 2–3) Students will explain that the purpose of advertising is to try to convince them to get their parents to buy them something and will demonstrate the ability to distinguish between advertising and content on websites.

Avoid the Impulse

Remember, What You Do Reflects on You

To make positive choices online, students must know how to engage in effective problem solving, watch out for "online traps" that could lead them to make a mistake, and evaluate possible options to make an ethical choice. In addition to this, students must know how to be a helpful ally. The problem-solving approach that is set forth in this chapter should permeate much of the other instruction, especially the instruction addressing digital aggression and relationship concerns.

To engage in effective problem solving requires an understanding of the actual risks. Thus, it is necessary to discuss the risks, without engaging in fearmongering. There are risks associated with crossing a busy street or riding a bike. There are risks online. Students need to understand the risks, and know how to protect themselves and to respond to negative situations. Keep it as simple as that.

The most effective way to stimulate these classroom discussions is to use real stories to illustrate the potential harmful consequences of online actions and foster effective problem solving that they can apply in situations they may be involved in or witness. The underlying focus of these discussions about stories should be on the following:

- *Considering motivations.* What might be motivating someone to act this way, or what might their personal motivations be in a similar situation?
  - Learning why people might act in a certain way helps in identifying possible options to find a positive resolution.

- *Assessing actual or possible consequences.* What was the consequence of an action taken, and was this good or bad? Or what are the possible consequences of other actions?
  - Focusing on actual or predictable consequences is an important strategy to address the fact that harmful consequences may be less evident in digital environments. Also, many times young people act impulsively, not stopping to consider the possible consequences of certain behaviors. Make sure they fully understand the predictable or possible consequences of actions taken when using digital technologies.
- *Identifying options for responses.* In every situation, students should be able to identify at least three options of actions that someone could take to resolve a similar situation, from the perspective of someone being in the situation and the perspective of someone witnessing the situation.
  - The issue is not finding the right solution because different situations may need to be addressed in different ways. The objective is to expand students' understandings of different things they could try, based on what is happening. Furthermore, they need to know that the first thing they try might not work. So they always need to have different options.
  - One of the options should be to ask an adult for assistance or report to an adult what they have witnessed. This option should be used if the situation is really serious and needs immediate attention or if what they have tried has not worked.

Encourage students to develop and practice scripts that can be used to guide what they say when they seek to respond or to intervene in a similar situation. These scripts should take all perspectives, responding to a negative situation, seeking to intervene in a negative situation, having someone suggest that someone stop engaging in at-risk or hurtful behavior, and so on.

There are different ways to practice this discussion of stories.

- *Complete stories that describe the entire incident.* In this analysis, everything has happened, and the story has come to a conclusion.
- *Set-up stories that describe a situation, but not the conclusion.* This practice leads to the steps they could follow if they get into or witness a similar situation.

There are many creative ways to obtain these stories:

- In advance of instruction, teachers can ask students to anonymously provide them with stories of actual incidents they have witnessed or been involved in. The reason this should be done in advance, rather than just asking students in class to describe such incidents, is to protect the privacy of students who might have been involved and whose identities could be revealed. If it is possible to anonymize these stories, they can be used for instructional purposes. Helpful illustrative anonymous stories from one class session can be saved or shared with other teachers.
- Pay attention to the news, especially any national news stories, as these can provide valuable teachable moments.
- The Cyber Savvy website at http://embracingdigitalyouth.org provides links to news stories and other stories that can be used to support classroom discussion. Teachers are invited to submit their own illustrative stories.
- If a specific incident has occurred in the school community that is generally well known, the confidentiality of students has likely already been breached. These incidents may provide an excellent teachable moment to discuss problem solving and decision making for future similar incidents. It will be important not to engage the students in a discussion of who was to blame. Instead, focus on possible motivations and ineffective decision making.

CRITICAL SKILLS

Problem Solving

Help students gain effective problem-solving skills. Here are some useful scenarios and related questions that can be asked.

- News story or complete scenario:
  - What appeared to initiate the situation? Who was involved? What was each person trying to accomplish? What did the participants fail to think about?
  - After the situation started to unfold, what decisions were made by the participants? What was the apparent motivation for those decisions?
  - What happened as a result of what each participant did? Was this a negative result or a positive outcome?
  - What other decisions could have been made by each participant? How could these other decisions have possibly changed the outcome?

- Scenario without a conclusion or an actual situation:
  - What is happening? Who is involved? What is each person trying to accomplish?
  - What might happen to each person involved? Would this be good or bad?
  - What are your personal standards and guidelines for your own actions if you were in a similar situation?
  - If you were in a similar situation, what are the possible things you could do? (Be sure to have at least three options, one of which is to ask for guidance from an adult.)

Online Traps

Help students learn to recognize online traps that can lead to bad choices.[1] These online traps include when students

- think they are invisible and so won't be caught;
- do not recognize that their online actions have harmed others or themselves, or have deceived others;
- act fast, especially when angry, and forget that the material posted in digital form can easily become very public and possibly permanent;
- follow others who make bad choices;
- think that because they can easily do something, it is okay;
- look for friends in the wrong places and find the wrong kinds of friends; and
- are being manipulated by a "creep."

Ethical Choices

Provide guidance on questions that students can ask themselves to make ethical choices.[2]

- How would I feel if someone did the same thing to me or to my best friend?
- What will other people think about me?
- What would my mom, dad, or other trusted adult think?
- Would this violate any agreements, rules, or laws?
- What would happen if everybody did this?
- How would this reflect on me?

---

[1] These traps are directly related to the influences discussed in Chapter 2.

[2] These questions are grounded in the positive influences discussed in Chapter 2.

Helpful Allies

Involve the students in identifying the important steps that they can take to act as a helpful ally.[3] These steps may include

- advising a peer who is engaging in a risky situation or ill-advised behavior;
- providing emotional support or problem-solving assistance to a peer who is possibly in a risky situation or is being hurt;
- privately confronting or publicly posting the hurtful actions of someone; and
- reporting serious or unresolved situations to a responsible adult.

For example, a recommended script for reaching out to privately confront someone who is engaging in hurtful or risky behavior might sound or look like this:

- Say stop: "You need to stop (describe behavior)."
- If appropriate, acknowledge the legitimacy of what this student is going through: "I know you just broke up . . ." "I know (name) can be irritating . . ." or "I know you think this person cares about you . . ."
- ". . . BUT": Describe reasons why this person's behavior is risky or inappropriate, using the following influence strategies.
  ○ Golden rule: If someone did this to you, you would not like it.
  ○ Social norms and reputation: Most students do not like to see someone being hurtful, so people are not going to like you or want to be friends with you.
  ○ Family values: Your parents would not approve of you doing this, and when they find out, they will be disappointed.
  ○ Violation of policy or rule: This is a violation of the school's policy, the terms of use of the site, and could be a violation of the law. If you are reported, you could get into trouble.
  ○ Risk of harm: This behavior could place you at risk of (describe possible consequence).
  ○ Evidence of manipulation: This person is engaging in behavior that is manipulative by (describe evidence of manipulation).
- Suggest restoration and positive future behavior: "I think you should apologize (publicly or privately depending on circumstances) and simply stay away from (name) if you can't get along." "You need to stop communicating with this person—just back off."

---

[3] This insight is grounded in the discussion regarding engaging witnesses set forth in Chapter 1 and the importance of this, as discussed in Chapter 3.

It may also be helpful to suggest creating a team of helpful allies. This can easily be accomplished using digital communication technologies. If material has been posted online that is hurtful, envision what might happen if not one but three students quickly post protests against such postings. Or envision how the person posting such material would respond if he or she received repeated messages from several other students protesting these actions. The members of the team could each use a different influence statement.

INSTRUCTIONAL OBJECTIVES

- (Grades 4–12) Students will recognize that any material they post or send in digital format can easily become public and potentially permanently available and that this can affect their reputations and relationships, and interfere with current or future opportunities—in a positive or negative manner.
- (Grades 4–12) Students will engage in effective problem solving to develop appropriate options for response to potentially harmful online situations, including an analysis of the situation, identification of potential harmful consequences, development of possible options for action, and evaluation of possible outcomes to those actions.
- (Grades 4–12) Students will determine the appropriateness of actions using digital technologies using self-reflection questions that will seek to address the potential negative influences on behavior and lead to safe, ethical, and responsible choices.
- (Grades 4–12) Students will recognize the key negative influences on behavior when using digital technologies—including the perception of invisibility; lack of tangible feedback; acting without thinking, which may result in posting damaging material in digital form; being negatively influenced by others; and thinking that because they can easily do something using technology, this gives them permission to do it—and describe strategies to avoid digital actions that have been negatively influenced.
- (Grades 4–12) Students will identify actions they can take to be a helpful ally if they witness a situation that could lead to a harmful consequence to another, including speaking out for good values, helping someone who is at risk or being harmed, and reporting significant or unresolved concerns to a responsible adult.

Read With Your Eyes Open

Assess the Credibility of Information

The ability to assess the credibility of information found online or sent digitally is an essential skill for success in the 21st century.[1] We have entered an era when anyone can post information online or send it digitally with no authority in place to approve or disapprove of the presentation of such information.

On the one hand, this could raise concerns about the degree of accuracy of the information presented. On the other hand, this allows for the publication of information that those in authority might not want to see made generally available.

This book is focused on digital safety and civility issues. Thus, the discussion of credibility is largely focused on digital safety aspects. The issue of assessing credibility in the context of academic studies is addressed because the same or very similar skills are applied to an assessment of safety. Thus, an objective in the delivery of instruction related to information credibility is also to tie this to a discussion related to safety, or vice versa.

School librarians will play an exceptionally important role in helping all teachers and students gain greater skills in media literacy and assessing the credibility of information. From a safety perspective, school librarians must understand how the skills in the assessment of credibility, which we will be addressing in the context of academic studies, also plays into digital safety issues. The important skills of discernment necessary to

---

[1] The MacArthur Foundation is providing incredible leadership in this arena through its Digital Media and Learning project: http://digitallearning.macfound.org/site/c.enJLKQNlFiG/b.2029199/k.94AC/Latest_News.htm

determine *credibility* are directly applicable to the determination of *trustworthiness*, the foundation for safe interactions with others online.

INFORMATION CREDIBILITY

Researchers supported by the MacArthur Foundation are conducting in-depth research around issues of information credibility and the challenges associated with teaching young people how to more effectively assess the credibility of information found online. There is much still to be learned in this area. A summary of the challenge in assessing the credibility of information found online was expressed very well in a recent MacArthur Foundation–funded publication titled *Digital Media, Youth, and Credibility*.

> With the sudden explosion of digital media content and access devices in the last generation, there is now more information available to more people from more sources than at any time in human history. Pockets of limited access by geography or status notwithstanding, people currently have ready access to almost inconceivably vast information repositories that are increasingly portable, accessible, and interactive in both delivery and formation. One result of this contemporary media landscape is that there exist incredible opportunities for learning, social connection, and individual entertainment and enhancement in a wide variety of forms. At the same time, however, the origin of information, its quality, and its veracity are in many cases less clear than ever before, resulting in an unparalleled burden on individuals to locate appropriate information and assess its meaning and relevance. Moreover, the same wide scale access and multiplicity of sources that ensure vast information availability also make assessing the credibility of information accurately extremely complex. It is also highly consequential: Assessing credibility inaccurately can have serious social, personal, educational, relational, health, and financial consequences.[2]

One helpful study assessed the ability of adult subjects to determine the credibility of websites in the context of concerns related to phishing—online schemes designed to trick people into providing financial information for identity theft.[3] The participants in the study were shown twenty

---

[2] Metzger, M., & Flanagin, A. (2007). *Digital media, youth, and credibility* (The MacArthur Series on Digital Media and Learning). Cambridge, MA: MIT Press. Summary retrieved June 22, 2011, from http://digitallearning.macfound.org/site/c.enJLKQNlFiG/b.2142779/k.A635/Credibility.htm

[3] Dhamija, R., Tygar, J. D., & Hearst, M. (2006). Why phishing works. In R. Grinter, T. Rodden, P. Aoki, E. Cutrell, R. Jeffries, & G. Olson (Eds.), *Proceedings of the SIGCHI conference on human factors in computing systems* (CHI '06) (pp. 581–590). New York, NY: ACM. Retrieved June 22, 2011, from http://portal .acm.org/citation.cfm?id=1124772.1124861

websites, only seven of which were legitimate, and asked to determine which were the legitimate sites. The participants knew that some of the sites that were presented to them were fake sites. The researchers found almost all participants were easily fooled.

There was, however, one participant in this study who was highly successful in determining which sites were the legitimate sites. His strategy was not based on an analysis of "what was on" the site, rather "how he got to" the site. He typed the name of the company into a search engine and then compared the site at the top of the search returns to the experimental site. This is a very important finding. It is easy for someone to produce a site that is credible in appearance. But it is much harder for someone to create a site that will be returned at or near the top of search results.

In the following information literacy guidelines, there will be a focus on effective strategies to get to credible sites, not simply an evaluation of what is on the sites. This also relates to safety issues when dealing with individuals or groups. The question of how this individual or group has come into your online life is a very important consideration.

THE IMPACT OF ATTEMPTED INFLUENCE

Many individuals, organizations, companies, and elected officials seek to influence our attitudes and behavior in the material they post online.[4] From the organizations we support, to the purchases we make, the people we elect, and the people we interact with, being able to identify when strategies are being used for the specific purpose of influencing our attitudes and behavior is very important.

Determining the credibility of online information is complicated by the fact that everyone—from credible, nonbiased information providers to "snake oil salesmen"—is using the same techniques to create sites and convey information in ways that appear to be highly credible.

Appearance of Credibility

Consumer Reports launched a Credibility Campaign to improve the trustworthiness of websites.[5] As part of this campaign, they established credibility guidelines that call for easy-to-find disclosures of site identity, ownership, policies on advertising, sponsorships, customer service, and privacy; they also call for a commitment to quickly and prominently correct wrong information. Sadly, when they did a study of how people assess the

---

[4] Two helpful resources to understand these issues better are: Cialdini, R. B. (2008). *Influence: Science and practice* (5th ed.). New York, NY: Prentice Hall; Jackson, B., & Jamieson, K. H. (2007). *UnSpun: Finding facts in a world of disinformation*. New York, NY: Random House.

[5] http://www.consumerWebwatch.org/Web-credibility.cfm

credibility of websites, they found that people did not look at these features. In fact, the study provided indications that are of significant concern:

> The data showed that the average consumer paid far more attention to the superficial aspects of a site, such as visual cues, than to its content. . . . Participants seemed to make their credibility-based decisions about the people or organization behind the site based upon the site's overall visual appeal. We had hoped to see people use more rigorous evaluation strategies while assessing sites.[6]

Students, whose level of cognitive development will make assessments such as this more challenging, are also likely inclined to make decisions about credibility of online information and the trustworthiness of individuals they meet online based on appearance, which can be deceiving. When dealing with individuals, this can be dangerous because unsafe people make a point of creating a positive appearance.

Search Engines

Students must recognize the commercial nature of search engines. Students must distinguish between search returns and ads and understand search-engine optimization. Companies selling products and advocacy organizations that try to influence opinion can use search-engine optimization techniques to make sure that their sites come up first in search returns.[7] Depending on the search, the top results in search returns could lead to sites that have a product or message to sell because those are the sites operated by organizations that have a strong interest in getting their message to the attention of more people.

However, search engines can also provide an excellent way to avoid scams. Most phishing scams involve e-mails or messages directing people to fake sites that have been set up to look like the real thing. What these fake sites cannot easily accomplish is achieving a high rank in a search engine.

Young people can also use search engines to investigate the safety and trustworthiness of individuals they might be interacting with by searching for additional information or postings. They can also search for independent reviews of companies or organizations.

---

[6] Fogg, B. J., Marable, L., Stanford, J., & Tauber, E. R. (2002). How do people evaluate a web site's credibility? *Consumer Reports WebWatch*. Retrieved June 22, 2011, from http://www.consumerwebwatch.org/dynamic/Web-credibility-reports-evaluate-abstract.cfm

[7] Search engine optimization. (n.d.). In *Wikipedia*. Retrieved June 22, 2011, from http://en.wikipedia.org/wiki/Search_engine_optimization

Contributory Editing Sites

Students should understand the issues related to sites that allow for contributory editing, such as on Wikipedia.[8] Articles on Wikipedia are only as credible as the people who have contributed to their creation. A helpful (and secure) article on the Wikipedia site outlines all of the ways in which people can commit what is called *vandalism* on the site— deliberate actions to compromise its integrity.[9] Wikipedia is constantly searching for better ways to ensure credibility within a user-contributed environment.

An additional issue of concern is grounded in the general societal perspective that information is not credible unless it has been vetted by an expert. This is associated with the larger social change that is shifting from an authority-based society to more of a network-based society.

According to a study published in 2005 by the journal *Nature*, Wikipedia is about as good a source of accurate information as the *Encyclopedia Britannica*—a stalwart in reliance on experts to establish credibility.[10] What has Britannica's response to Wikipedia been? In 2008, Britannica announced a new approach that solicits more active online involvement of experts and readers.[11]

Thus, it appears that while Wikipedia has been active in developing strategies to achieve a higher degree of credibility within a user-contributory environment, Britannica has been moving toward greater reliance on user contributions.

STRATEGIES TO ASSESS CREDIBILITY AND SAFETY

The following are strategies for assessing credibility, with a focus on safety. Note that these strategies are set forth in pairs. The first strategy is most relevant to issues of credibility. The second strategy applies this approach to issues of the safety and trustworthiness of a person or group.

---

[8] http://www.wikipedia.org

[9] Wikipedia:Vandalism. (n.d.). In *Wikipedia*. Retrieved June 22, 2011, from http://en.wikipedia.org/wiki/Wikipedia:Vandalism

[10] Terdiman, D. (2005, December 15). Study: Wikipedia as accurate as Britannica. *CNET News*. Retrieved June 22, 2011, from http://news.cnet.com/Study-Wikipedia-as-accurate-as-Britannica/2100-1038_3-5997332.html

[11] Britannica Editors. (2008, June 3). Britannica's new site: More participation, collaboration from experts and readers. *Encyclopedia Britannica Blog*. Retrieved June 22, 2011, from http://www.britannica.com/blogs/2008/06/britannicas-new-site-more-participation-collaboration-from-experts-and-readers/

Determine Importance

- Consider how important it is that the information, site, or individual be credible.
  - Information searches vary in importance, and thus the need to pay attention to credibility varies. Consider the importance of determining the credibility of a site that provides health information as compared to information about a new movie.
- Consider how important it is that the individual or group be safe and trustworthy.
  - The degree of care necessary if they are interacting with an individual in a public group is different from the degree of care necessary when deciding whether to allow this individual to have access to their personal profile. Different kinds of groups will require a different degree of care. Consider how closely they will be interacting with this individual and what access this individual will have to their personal information.

Consider Path

- Reflect on how you got to any site.
  - If you get to a site following a link from a site that already has credibility, such as a list of good research sites for students provided by an education group, it is likely that the site is credible. Sites found through a search engine will vary in quality and credibility. A link provided in an e-mail message from an unknown individual is less likely to lead to a credible site.
- Reflect on how you came into contact with an individual or group.
  - Is the individual a friend of a trusted friend, and can your friend verify the trustworthiness of this individual? Have you interacted with this individual in a public forum for a sufficient period of time to have formed an "informed" opinion of this individual's safety? Have you found this individual or group, or did this individual or someone from a group reach out to you? Why?

Evaluate Source

- Evaluate the source of the information and what other people think of this source.
  - Is there independent evidence of the expertise and credibility of the source? Type the site name in quotes, without using http://, in a search engine to determine who links to the site.
- Evaluate the safety of the individual or group by reviewing postings.

○ Look closely at the material this person has posted. Note whether there are inconsistencies or evidence of concerns related to personal values. Also look at who this person associates with and make a determination of the safety of these individuals.

Assess Interest and Possible Bias

- Look for evidence of bias or personal interest, especially if the issue is a controversial public matter or the site is seeking to sell something.
  - ○ Does the material appear to provide information, or is the site trying to convince visitors to take some kind of action? Is there any evidence of self-serving, such as a source of funding? Is it advocating for a cause or selling products or services?
- Consider the personal interests and possible biases of any individual or group with whom they are interacting.
  - ○ Is this an individual who desires a friendship relationship based on safe mutual interests, or is there a possibility of other interests? What are the objectives of any group?

Assess the Consistency of the Information

- Determine whether the information is consistent with information found through other sources.
  - ○ Is the same or similar information present at several locations? Or is information conflicting? What is the basis of the conflict?
- Determine whether the individual or group you are communicating with is providing consistent information.
  - ○ Is what this individual is communicating consistent with other material that this person has posted and information within his or her circle of friends? Is what the participants in a group are communicating consistent with other trustworthy information?

Look for Evidence of Influence or Manipulation

- Determine whether there is evidence that the site is using techniques that are known to be used in attempt to influence attitudes and behavior.
  - ○ Is the site offering coupons or other benefits in exchange for providing personal information? Is the site encouraging users to sign up, either to receive messages or establish a friendship link, for the purposes of soliciting commitment? Is your assessment of the site being influenced by its appearance or its

presentation as an authority, and is this assessment justified by other factors? Is the site suggesting that users must engage in some action quickly or else lose out?

- Determine whether there is evidence that the individual or group is using techniques that are known to be used for manipulation.
    - Is the individual or group showering you with compliments, offers of opportunities, gifts, and favors? Is the individual or group encouraging a personal commitment? Is the individual or group threatening some loss if you do not act in a certain way?

Conduct a Substantive Evaluation

- Evaluate the information itself.
    - Is it logical? Is it consistent with what you already know is true? Does it "feel" right? Or do you have a gut reaction that there is a concern?
- Evaluate the safety of the individual or group.
    - Does this individual or group share the values that are known to support safe and responsible attitudes and behavior? Does this individual or group feel right? Or do they have a gut reaction that there is a concern?

Consult With Others

- Ask for the opinions of others about the accuracy of information found on a site, especially a parent, teacher, or librarian.
    - What do they think of the credibility of the information and source?
- Ask for the opinions of others about their perceptions of the trustworthiness of someone you have been interacting with online, especially a friend, parent, or other trusted adult.
    - What do they think about the safety of this individual or group?

INSTRUCTIONAL ACTIVITIES

The instructional objectives addressed in this chapter will also need to permeate the instructional activities in other areas. A student checklist could be created for any assignment that involves online research. Students could be encouraged to find negative and positive examples illustrating sites that appear to be credible and those that require more investigation.

INSTRUCTIONAL OBJECTIVES

- (Grades 4–12) Students will understand that the skills that they gain to assess the credibility of information found on websites also apply to assessing the safety and trustworthiness of individuals or groups they interact with through digital communications.
- (Grades 4–12) Students will recognize that any individual, organization, or company can post information online; that the intentions of posting such information may vary; that sometimes a variety of individuals, organizations, or companies may be contributing to the information presented; and that there is no mechanism to assure the credibility of such information.
- (Grades 4–12) Students will understand the dangers in relying on appearance and high ranking in search returns as a basis to assess credibility.
- (Grades 4–12) Students will demonstrate skills in assessing the credibility of information and the safety and trustworthiness of individuals, including
  - assessing the importance of determining credibility and safety;
  - considering the path to the information;
  - evaluating the source;
  - looking for evidence of interest and potential bias;
  - determining the consistency of the information;
  - looking for evidence of influence or manipulation;
  - conducting a substantive evaluation; and
  - consulting with others.

Keep Your Life in Balance

Avoid Addictive Use

Addictive use is an excessive amount of time spent using digital technologies, resulting in lack of healthy engagement in other areas of life. Addictive use appears to be similar to other recognized behavioral addictions.

The research on time spent involved with digital communication and psychosocial concerns is somewhat mixed. Some research has indicated that young people who are very active when using digital technologies are also very engaged in school and other activities.[1] They appear to be highly social young people whose use of technology has been incorporated into their social activities.

But other research has shown a connection between an excessive amount of digital activity and depression, social anxiety, and suicidal ideation.[2] Spending an excessive time online has also been correlated with other risk factors. Note that correlation means that both aspects are present, not necessarily that one is causing another. Note also that a high amount of use does not equate with addictive access. There also must be other resulting harm.

---

[1] Lenhart, A., Madden, M., Rankin, A., & Smith, A. (2007). *Teens and social media: The use of social media gains a greater foothold in teen life as email continues to lose its luster.* Pew Internet & American Life Project. Retrieved June 22, 2011, from http://www.pewinternet.org/Reports/2007/Teens-and-Social-Media.aspx

[2] Kim, K., Ryu, E., Chon, M., Yeun, E., Choi, S., Seo, J., & Nam, B.-W. (2006). Internet addiction in Korean adolescents and its relation to depression and suicidal ideation: A questionnaire survey. *International Journal of Nursing Studies, 43*, 185–192: The levels of depression and suicide ideation were highest in the Internet-addicts group; Jenaro, C., Flores, N., Mez-vela, M., Gonza, F., Gil, L., & Caballo, C. (2007). Problematic Internet and cell-phone use: Psychological, behavioral, and health correlates. *Addiction Research and Theory. 15*(3), 309–320: Heavy Internet use is associated with high anxiety, and high cell-phone use is associated to being female, and having high anxiety and insomnia.

The American Psychiatric Association (APA) recently noted that Internet addiction appears to be a common disorder that merits inclusion in the *Diagnostic and Statistical Manual of Mental Disorders*, or *DSM*.[3] The APA outlined factors that need to be considered to determine whether excessive use has become addictive use:

> Internet addiction appears to be a common disorder that merits inclusion in DSM-V. Conceptually, the diagnosis is a compulsive-impulsive spectrum disorder that involves online and/or offline computer usage and consists of at least three subtypes: excessive gaming, sexual preoccupations, and e-mail/text messaging. All of the variants share the following four components: 1) excessive use, often associated with a loss of sense of time or a neglect of basic drives, 2) withdrawal, including feelings of anger, tension, and/or depression when the computer is inaccessible, 3) tolerance, including the need for better computer equipment, more software, or more hours of use, and 4) negative repercussions, including arguments, lying, poor achievement, social isolation, and fatigue.[4]

Instructionally, there are two key objectives. Help students

- recognize when their use of digital technologies is excessive and has crossed the line to an interference with other life activities, which include
  - spending more time more time online than planned;
  - using the Internet or cell phone late into the night;
  - fatigue due to lack of sleep;
  - spending time online instead of other activities, especially in-person activities with friends;
  - being preoccupied with online activities when not using technologies;
  - feeling depressed or anxious, especially if not using digital technologies;
  - arguing with parents about time limits or activities; and
  - using sneak ways to get around parent restrictions.
- identify strategies they can use to keep their life in balance, such as
  - setting goals for the amount of time they will spend online and keep track of their time;
  - making a commitment to spend more time with their friends having fun that does not involve screens;

---

[3] Block, J. J. (2008, March). Issues for DSM-V: Internet addiction. *American Journal of Psychiatry, 165*, 306–307. Retrieved June 22, 2011, from http://ajp.psychiatryonline.org/cgi/content/full/165/3/306

[4] Id.

- avoiding surfing, gabbing, or gaming when doing homework—
they should set a goal to complete a certain portion and then
give themselves a short reward break; and
- turning their cell phone off at night.

INSTRUCTIONAL ACTIVITIES

Two instructional activities are recommended. One is to have the students
anonymously complete the Cyber Savvy Balance of Life survey found at
http://embracingdigitalyouth.org. Then analyze and discuss their findings.
By identifying the normative data for the student in the class, or a group of
classes, hopefully those students whose usage is excessive in comparison will
realize the need for change. The students could then be asked to write a brief
essay or create some form of message related to keeping their life in balance.

The other suggestion is to follow the guidance of a university profes-
sor who challenged her students to take twenty-four hours to unplug from
all media—with the exception of a class blog where they could write their
impressions.[5] This project, called "24 Hours Unplugged: A Day Without
Media," provided some excellent insight into how these college students
were using media. To focus in on more of the Internet and texting issues,
a middle school or high school day might simply be a day without texting
and the Internet and the requirement to keep a written journal.

INSTRUCTIONAL OBJECTIVES

- (Grades 4–12) Students will identify indicators that can
determine whether the amount of time they spend using
digital devices is interfering with other important activities.
Indicators include spending more time more time online
than planned; using Internet late into the night; fatigue;
spending time online instead of other activities; being preoccupied with online activities; depression or anxiety; arguing about time limits; and sneaking around parent limits.
- (Grades 4–12) Students will describe strategies they can use
to keep their time using digital devices in balance with other
important life activities, including setting goals and keeping
track of time, making plans for other activities, avoiding
being online when doing homework, and turning cell phone
off at night.

---

[5] http://withoutmedia.wordpress.com/

Think Before You Post

Protect Your Reputation and Respect Others

Some young people appear to be unaware that online postings, information, or photos, even if shared privately, can become public, and that people will judge them—either positively or negatively—based on their digital appearance, also called their *digital footprint*. If their digital footprint demonstrates evidence of poor judgment, this can place them at risk or damage their reputation, friendships, and current or future opportunities.

Introduce students to the Internet Law of Predictable Consequences:

> The more embarrassing, outrageous, or damaging the material you post or send privately, the more likely it will become very public and be seen by people who will judge you badly. Alternatively, a digital footprint that provides an excellent demonstration of their skills, interests, and personal values can contribute in very effective ways to their success in making friends and gaining positive opportunities.

Most tweens and teens post information on social networking sites. One of the most important steps in protecting personal information is using the privacy protection features on these sites. It is very important to emphasize that "limited to friends" does not mean "private"—not if they have more than one friend.

Students should know that if they send material privately to a friend, this information could still be made public through inadvertent or intentional action by the recipient. Friends might not know that they want to keep this information private and simply share without intending to cause any harm. Or a relationship might deteriorate and a former friend may have embarrassing information that is then sent with the intention to cause harm. Mistakes can also be made. Failing to log out if using a private profile on a public computer, or simply letting a friend borrow a cell phone, could result in private information or photos being shared.

DIFFERENT TYPES OF INFORMATION, RISKS, AND PROTECTION STRATEGIES

Students must know that there are different kinds of information about themselves or others that could be posted, different places where this information might be shared, and different individuals who might receive or be able to access this information. The risks are associated with the kind of information shared and the people with whom it is shared. The following are the kinds of information that can be shared, issues related to this material, and protection strategies.

Personal Interest Material

- *Material that provides insight into students' interests and activities and who they are as people.* This kind of material is generally safe to share on protected profiles on safe social networking sites, as well as other community sites. Students must be aware that this kind of material will be gathered within the context of a market profile, which will be used to direct advertising to them.
  - ○ Share with care.

Personal Contact Information

- *Information such as an address, phone numbers, and e-mail/IM addresses.* If personal contact information is disclosed, this could make it easier for an unsafe person to contact them or for the information to be used to send them advertising. Do not use a threat that a predator may track them down and abduct them—this is not happening. However, there is a concern about home theft if their address is readily available and they post information about a time their family will be away from the house. There are perfectly appropriate reasons to provide this kind of information online, such as for a purchase.
  - ○ Do not publicly post this kind of contact information in any profile. It may be appropriate to privately share this with selected individuals or on websites with appropriate privacy policies. Younger students should always consult with parents before sharing contact information.

Financial Identity Information

- *Any personal identification or financial account information, including birth dates.* This information can be used for identity theft. Disclosing an actual birth date and home town can allow identity thieves to determine their social security number, which can be used for identity theft.[1]
  - ○ Financial identity information should only be shared with a parent's permission on secure websites, such as when making a purchase. Do not publicly provide an accurate birth date.

Sensitive or Damaging Personal Material

- *Material that could make them appear vulnerable or demonstrate that they make bad choices, or simply any information they want to be kept secret.* This specifically includes provocative photos. The risks associated with this kind of material are that it could be used to manipulate them or harm their reputation, or could attract unsafe individuals.
  - ○ This material generally should never be posted or shared, either publicly or privately. However, it is safe to discuss sensitive material on a professional support site hosted by a legitimate organization. Being realistic, most teens will share this kind of information privately with trusted friends. They must be aware of the potential risks—and judge the trustworthiness of their friends carefully. They should not simply assume their friend will understand the need to keep information confidential. If they share something they want kept secret, they should specifically state this.

Sensitive or Damaging Material About Others

- *Material posted by one person that could make another person appear vulnerable, evidence that he or she makes negative choices, or any material this other person would want to be kept secret.*
  - ○ In addressing this issue, it will likely be helpful to place a strong reliance on a Golden Rule norm of not posting material about others if you would not want similar material about you to be posted.

---

[1] Leggett, H. (2009, July 6) Social security numbers deduced from public data. *Wired.* Retrieved June 22, 2011, from http://www.wired.com/wiredscience/2009/07/predictingssn/

Sensitive or Damaging Material About Them Posted by Others

- *Material posted by someone else that could harm their reputation, friendships, and future opportunities.* This is a form of cyberbullying that will be addressed in Chapter 19.
  - Younger students should simply be advised to tell an adult. Older students may demand this material be removed, file an abuse report (which, unfortunately, may or may not be effective), and report serious or unresolved situations to a responsible adult.

Threatening Material

- *Threatening material that indicates intent to harm someone or oneself.* These threats or distressing material could be real or not. It is best to assume this is a legitimate concern.
  - This concern is also addressed in Chapter 19. Briefly, students should know to never post material that someone might think is a threat, because this could lead someone to believe it is real and could lead to significant trouble, including arrest. Also, they should always immediately report material that raises concerns about a threatening situation, because if the threat is real and not reported, someone could get hurt.

INSTRUCTIONAL ACTIVITIES

The "Think Before You Post" lessons will also emerge in the context of several other areas, including scams, social networking safety, cyberbullying, and risky relationship issues. Additional issues that are important to address in the context of information shared about others or information shared about them relate to legal dimensions of such postings, including criminal laws, and civil torts.

Look for examples of news stories where people have had very damaging things or very positive things happen to them simply based on the materials they have posted online, and use these as the basis for discussions. Encourage students to enunciate their personal standards for the material they will send privately or post publicly. Ideally, this statement will reflect an understanding of the risks or ethical issues associated with sharing each kind of material. Sending this personal statement home to have it signed by parents could be an effective outreach strategy that will also increase parental understanding of these issues.

One instructional strategy is to have students create a three-part table like this: Column 1—Types of information; Column 2—Risks and ethical issues associated with sharing; Column 3—Protection and response strategies. Students could add to this table by finding news stories or other examples that illustrate these risks.

A creative activity would include making a poster or computer-screen design on some variation of this theme: "If you wouldn't (fill in the blank) don't post it or send it digitally." Students could be encouraged to think of issues related to their personal reputation or respect for the rights of others in creating this statement.

INSTRUCTIONAL OBJECTIVES

Teachers will note a difference in approach in the instructional objectives on these issues between middle and high school. The reason for this difference is the perspective that high school students will take on more personal responsibility for such information sharing.

- (Grades 4–12) Students will recognize that any material they post or send in digital format can easily become very public, potentially permanently available, and can potentially affect their reputation, relationships, and current or future opportunities—in a positive or negative manner.
- (Grades 4–12) Students will distinguish different kinds of personal information about themselves or others, recognize the risks associated with disclosure of such information, identify different kinds of online environments where such information might be disclosed, identify possible recipients of such information, and demonstrate effective strategies to protect against disclosure of personal information in a manner that could cause harm to reputation or opportunities.
  - (Grades 4–12) Personal interest material includes interests and activities. This is generally safe to share on protected profiles or on safe online community sites. Such material could be used to direct advertising to them.
  - (Grades 4–8) Personal contact information includes address, phone numbers, and e-mail/IM address. This could make it easier for an unsafe person to find them or be used to send them advertising. This information should not be posted or shared without parent permission.

(Grades 9–12) This material should not be posted in an online profile. This material should never be shared with an online stranger. Only provide on it web forms for necessary purposes such as a purchase, when privacy will be protected.

○ (Grades 4–12) Financial identity includes any personal identification or financial account information, as well as hometown and birth date. This can be used for identity theft and should only be shared with a parent's permission on secure websites.

○ (Grades 4–12) Sensitive or damaging personal material includes material that can make them appear vulnerable or demonstrate that they make negative choices, or any information they want to be kept secret. This could be used to manipulate them or disseminated to harm their reputation, relationships, and future opportunities. This information should generally never be posted or shared publicly or privately. Sensitive information may be shared with care on a professional support site or with a very trustworthy friend.

○ (Grades 4–12) Sensitive or damaging personal material about others could harm their reputation, relationships, and future opportunities. This material should never be shared publicly or privately.

○ (Grades 4–8) Damaging information about them posted by others could harm their reputation and opportunities. Tell a responsible adult. (Grades 9–12) Damaging information about them posted by others could harm their reputation and opportunities. Demand it be removed. File a complaint with the site. If it is serious or not removed, tell an adult.

○ (Grades 4–12) Threats could be real or not. Never post material that someone might think is a threat. Always report a possible threatening situation because if it is real, someone could get hurt.

Connect Safely

Interact Safely With Others Online

Young people can be expected to interact with friends, acquaintances, friends of friends, and strangers. Any can be safe—or present a risk. Anyone the young person does not know very well in person requires special consideration. People who are not known—or are not known very well—present greater risks because they can more easily be deceptive online, and it is more difficult to recognize this deception.

PUBLIC OR PERSONAL

Young people must distinguish between public communication environments and personal communications.

- Public environments are places where many people engage in communications. This includes gaming sites, discussion forums, chat rooms, and the like. Their safety depends largely on the kind of site.
- Private communications include e-mail, IM or private chats, social networking messaging, and texting. Their safety depends largely on the person with whom the young person is communicating.

Emphasize to students the importance of exercising significant care related to who they allow into their personal communications environment, especially who they accept as a friend on a social networking site. Most students will already have figured this out, and likely will have experiences or strategies to share. Younger students should only friend someone they know and trust. Slightly older students should limit their connections to people they know and people whom a trusted friend knows in person. Many of them already have these personal standards, so it is possible to rely on a positive social-norms approach to encourage this. Eventually, older students may also add people they have met in some other online venue.

There are two common rationales that students often note when making a decision on whom to allow into their personal-communications environment. One is the avoidance of a negative outcome: "To avoid having to deal with creeps." The other is to achieve a positive outcome: "So only the people I know and trust can see my personal information." It should be possible to easily elicit these rationales from students in discussion.

UNCOMFORTABLE OR HURTFUL

If younger students, Grades 4–7, are careful in limiting their personal communications to known people, likely the greatest concerns are related to communicating with someone on a public entertainment site who is making them feel uncomfortable or is being hurtful.

Likely the best words students this age will use to describe someone who is making them feel uncomfortable are *weird* or *creep*. People who are hurtful could be anyone, including people they know.

Elicit from them some examples of when they have interacted with someone who has made them feel this way. Indicate that this is an important lesson in learning to trust their gut when someone is making them feel uncomfortable and in learning the importance of leaving that kind of situation. Then ask how they responded. Likely the vast majority will tell you they simply ignored the person or left the site. Remind them that if this did not work to stop the contact, or if they still felt uncomfortable, they should talk to a responsible adult.

DIGITAL NASTIES

The overwhelming majority of individuals teens will interact with online are safe. But they could run into "nasty" online people, especially in their expanded interactions on social networking or gaming sites. The following are the more typical kinds of digital nasties.

Posers

People who post material about themselves that is not true are posers. This is generally only possible for someone who is not known—or not known well. Many times, teens will share information that is not totally accurate, which is to be expected as they are exploring new aspects of their emerging personal identity. So a little "posing," if not done for harmful purposes, is of no significant concern. The concern comes if the person who is posing is also trying to manipulate a young person.

- Take time to get to know people online. Carefully review postings, recognizing that the information shared could be false. Watch out for inconsistencies. Trust your gut, because when someone tells you something that is not quite right, it will usually make you feel uncomfortable.

Impersonators

Impersonators are people who break into someone's account or create a fake profile to send messages or post material that will damage the reputation of the person depicted. Students must watch out for impersonators who might have impersonated them, as well as those who have broken into accounts of someone they know.

- Select a safe password and protect your passwords by not sharing with others or using them when others might figure them out. If someone has broken into your account or has set up an account or profile, file an abuse report with the site and alert your friends that someone is impersonating them, so that others who might see the material posted will understand what is happening. If someone has impersonated a friend, immediately alert your friend and others, and file an abuse report.

Fakes

People may set up false profiles to trick and humiliate someone. A clear indicator of a potential concern is the profile of someone who seems not to be regularly communicating with a group of friends who this person knows face-to-face.

- Watch out for that "hot teen" who none of your trustworthy friends know face-to-face who appears to be overly eager to form a relationship with you.

Griefers or Trolls

People who join games or other groups for the sole purpose of interfering with the enjoyment of others, to cause grief, are known as *griefers* or *trolls*.[1] If someone responds with argument, anger, or a counterattack, this is just what the griefer or troll wants.

---

[1] Griefer. (n.d.). In *Wikipedia*. Retrieved June 22, 2011, from http://en.wikipedia.org/wiki/Griefer

- Ignore or block griefers and trolls, leave the area or site, or file an abuse report.

Creeps

Creeps are people who try to manipulate young people into doing something that will end up hurting or humiliating them. Most teens appear to have a pretty good "creep monitor." Creeps often send overly friendly messages and are overly eager to form a relationship. They tell the young person how hot he or she is, offer gifts or opportunities, try to push them into a special secret relationship, ask for a sexy photo, and try to turn them against their parents or friends. Very frequently, creeps try to obtain a nude photo or convince the teen to engage in a sexual encounter.[2] The very important insight that all teens must have is that creeps can be very dangerous, not only to them but also to other teens.

- Anytime anyone you are interacting with online—known in person or not—is being overly friendly and overly eager, this should send up a red flag. Tell an adult.

Downers

People or groups that encourage harmful things like anorexia, self-cutting, hate, or gang activity are called *downers*. These kinds of people or groups provide emotional support to vulnerable teens—at a very harmful price. Vulnerable teens who are looking for friends online may end up finding the wrong kinds of friends.

There are online communities and websites that support unsafe activities or encourage dangerous activities. Unsafe communities focus on actions that can cause self-harm, including those that support self-cutting, anorexia and bulimia, steroid use, drug use, passing-out games, suicide, and other similar unsafe activities.[3] Dangerous groups promote actions that could cause harm to others, including hate sites and groups, gangs, and other troublesome youth groups, including groups of local youth, hacker communities, and groups that exchange pornography and discuss pedophilia.[4]

---

[2] This is discussed more in Chapter 20.

[3] Whitlock, J. L., Powers, J. L., & Eckenrode, J. (2006). The virtual cutting edge: The Internet and adolescent self-injury. *Developmental Psychology, 42*(3), 407–417. See also Mitchell, K., & Ybarra, M. (2007). Online behavior of youth who engage in self-harm provides clues for preventive intervention. *Preventive Medicine, 45*, 392–396. Retrieved June 22, 2011, from http://www.unh.edu/ccrc/pdf/CV160.pdf

[4] Anti-Defamation League. (n.d.). Poisoning the web: Hatred online. Internet bigotry, extremism and violence. Retrieved June 22, 2011, from http://www.adl.org/poisoning_web/introduction.asp; Wolf, C. (2000). Racist, bigots, and the law on the Internet. *GigaLaw.com*. Retrieved June 22, 2011, from http://www.adl.org/internet/internet_law1.asp; National Alliance of Gang Investigators Associations. (2005.) *2005 national gang threat assessment.* Retrieved June 22, 2011, from http://www.ojp.usdoj.gov/BJA/what/2005_threat_assesment.pdf

Harmful groups provide strong emotional support for marginalized youth.[5] The groups often include older teens and adults who act as mentors. The groups adopt symbols to foster group identity. Online rituals are used to solicit evidence that the participant is truly committed to the ideals of the group. The groups will exclude anyone deemed not to abide by the group norms, which will act to reinforce the importance of abiding by those norms to remain connected and receive support.

- Research on this concern is just emerging. These groups will only attract a minority of youth whose concerns probably are best addressed in the context of targeted risk prevention and intervention. Recognize that not all online communities in which vulnerable teens participate are harmful. Marginalized youth may find a very healthy online environment where they fit in with people who have their own interests. Likely it is not advisable to spend much time exploring these groups, as this could lead more at risk students to look into these communities or groups. Therefore, the message should be kept more general, related to the need to carefully consider the values and standards of groups of people they interact with online, and the need that, if a friend appears to be interacting with a group of people who are not making positive choices, they should likely raise these concerns to a responsible adult.

MEETING IN PERSON

Sometimes teens will want to meet in person with someone they have gotten to know online. In the vast majority of these situations, this is just a meeting with another teen, generally a friend of a friend. But these situations could present risk, so there is a need to be careful.

A recent EU Kids Online survey asked young people about these meetings.[6] Nine percent of these youth met in person with someone who they had gotten to know online. Of these, 57 percent met with a friend of a friend, and only 11 percent of those who met with someone were bothered or upset, which included a range from very upset to just a little upset. Based on this data, it appears that there is a one in ten chance that getting together in person with someone you have gotten to know online could lead to an unpleasant situation. Thus, there is a need to exercise caution because sometimes meeting in person could result in a negative situation.

---

[5] Pascoe, C. J. (2008, January 22). "You're just another fatty": Creating a pro-Ana subculture online. *Digital Youth Research.* Retrieved June 22, 2011, from http://digitalyouth.ischool.berkeley.edu/node/104

[6] Livingstone et al., supra.

If we just tell teens "no," some may meet anyway and may not take steps to be safe. They need to know how to meet safely. Especially in high school, they are unlikely to take a parent to such meeting but will willingly bring a friend.

Meeting safely includes some important steps:

- Have a parent and friends look over this person's profile to see if they detect any signs of concern.
- Meet in a public place, like an eating section at the shopping mall.
- Bring along some trusted friends and, if younger, have a parent nearby.
- Make sure to have a well-thought-out "escape" plan.
- Have parent approval, as well as the approval of the friend's parents.
- Never leave the public place with this person.

INSTRUCTIONAL APPROACHES

The use of insight into students' positive social norms and practices should be very helpful in these discussions, as are scenarios where students have come into connection with a "digital nasty."

One recommended instructional activity is to have students create a two-page document or slide presentation. The first page would have a story about someone unsafe whom they, or a friend, had run into online. A picture or illustration might also be appropriate. The second page would set out

- strategies to prevent attracting or engaging with this kind of person,
- signs that someone might not be safe,
- three things that they can do if they recognize they are interacting with someone who might not be safe, and
- what they could say to their friend if it appears their friend is interacting with someone who is unsafe.

INSTRUCTIONAL OBJECTIVES

- (Grades 4–12) Students will describe the differences between public and private communication environments in terms of the kinds of people they may interact with in these environments and the risks associated with these interactions, and describe basic safety practices for interacting with people through both public and private communications.

(Continued)

(Continued)

- (Grades 4–12) Students will know that if someone they are interacting with is making them feel uncomfortable (by being overly friendly or overly pushy, by acting in a strange manner, or by being hurtful), they should discontinue contact by leaving the site or blocking the person and, if appropriate, file an abuse report. Students will know the importance of reporting to a responsible adult in situations where someone appears to present a danger to anyone, if they are unable to stop contact, or if they continue to feel uncomfortable.

- (Grades 4–7) Students will recognize the dangers presented when interacting with someone online who is not known face-to-face; they should communicate with friends only in personal communications, and others only on safe youth sites.

- (Grades 8–12) Students will recognize the dangers presented when interacting with someone online who is not known well in person, including acquaintances, friends of friends, and strangers. Students will explain safe practices for interacting with these different kinds of people, including safe personal standards for when they will friend someone in their personal-communication environment. Generally, students will know the importance of limiting communications in personal communication environments to only people whom they know or a trusted friend knows in person.

- (Grades 8–12) Students will recognize the importance of exercising care when getting to know people online and recognize the risks presented by others who are presenting false information, may try to impersonate them, have created a fake profile, are causing grief, may be trying to manipulate them, or may be trying to encourage involvement in unsafe actions.

- (Grades 4–12) Students will recognize the potential risks of meeting in person with someone whom they have gotten to know online and describe steps to take to arrange for a safe meeting, including having someone they trust review this person's profile and communications, meeting in a public place with a parent or friends present, having a well-designed escape plan, obtaining parental approval, and not leaving with this person.

Keep Yourself Secure

Implement Security and Avoid Scams

Parents should take the responsibility to ensure the security of home computers. Given young people's advanced technical skills and behavior that could lead to security concerns, it makes sense to involve them in the activities necessary to maintain security. High school students should gain this insight in preparation for adulthood. The security concerns include online scammers, hackers, and identity thieves who could access their computer, personal information, finances, and more. The Federal Trade Commission's (FTC) OnGuard Online site also has excellent resources addressing these issues, including a reproducible handout that can be downloaded to provide very helpful for instruction, especially at the high school level.[1]

IDENTIFY THEFT AND PHISHING

Identity theft occurs when criminals obtain financial or identity information that allows them to steal another person's identity to commit financial theft.[2] According to the FTC, millions of people become victims of identity theft every year. Teens may think this does not include them, but it does. Have them do a search on the terms *teens* and *identity theft*, and this will enlighten them.

---

[1] http://www.onguardonline.gov

[2] Federal Trade Commission. (n.d.). About identity theft. *Fighting Back Against Identity Theft*. Retrieved June 22, 2011, from http://www.ftc.gov/bcp/edu/microsites/idtheft/consumers/about-identity-theft.html

There are many ways to obtain the financial information necessary to commit identity theft, but a popular way online is to engage in *phishing*. Criminals who engage in phishing send out e-mails, texts, or other messages that tell the recipient to click to a website or call a phone number to update their account information or claim a prize. Messages related to updating accounts often suggest something bad will happen, such as loss of the account, if the person doesn't respond quickly with the requested personal information. It is very easy for criminals engaged in phishing to set up sites that look very similar to legitimate business sites.

Strategies from the FTC to avoid phishing scams include the following:

- Never reply to an e-mail, text, or pop-up message that asks for personal or financial information, or click on links in the message. Legitimate businesses simply do not send out messages like this.
- Don't provide personal or financial information through a site until you have checked for indicators that the site is secure, like a lock icon on the browser's status bar or a website URL that begins with "https:" (the "s" stands for *secure*). But realize that criminals can even forge these indicators.
- To make a purchase from a site that you have any questions about, first call the phone number to see if this is a legitimate business. Also, when interacting with a lesser-known business, type the name of the company in a search engine to see what information might be available.

Another strategy to avoid accessing a scam site is to type the name of the bank or commercial site in a search engine and then access the site from the search returns. It is impossible for a scam site to get to the top of a search engine return.

ONLINE SHOPPING

- Criminals can gain access to databases of personal information by hacking into those databases.[3] This is why it is very important to be especially careful whenever providing personal financial information on any site—especially one that is unknown or may be less sophisticated and therefore have lax security. Students should know the importance of researching any site carefully before providing any financial information to make sure they are

---

[3] Online shopping. (2008, February). *OnGuard Online: Quick Facts*. Retrieved June 22, 2011, from http://www.onguardonline.gov/topics/online-shopping.aspx

dealing with a legitimate source. Additionally, they should never provide an online payment using a debit card. A debit card links to a specific bank account, so there is greater vulnerability. There are also greater protections under federal law for credit card fraud. In the event something goes wrong, if they use a credit card, they are protected under the Federal Fair Credit Billing Act, which provides the right to dispute charges on their credit card.[4]

FILE SHARING/PEER-TO-PEER NETWORKING

File-sharing software, also called *peer-to-peer (P2P) networking software*, can provide users with access to files on other people's computers.[5] When people download special software, this connects their computer to an informal network of other computers running the same software. The software is free and easy to access.

File sharing presents a significant number of concerns:

- If not configured properly, all files on their computer may be accessible—possibly including files that have personal financial information.
- Frequently, when people download files, they end up downloading malware, which can infect their computer and allow criminals to have access to their files.
- P2P networking software is often used to distribute pornography, including illegal child pornography.[6]

COMPUTER SECURITY

High school students should learn the basics of maintaining computer security by keeping the security software active and updating it regularly.[7] Computers should have antivirus and antispyware software, as well as a firewall. Security software protects against the newest threats only if it is up to date. It is also important to obtain security software from legitimate vendors. Some criminals distribute malware disguised as antispyware software. They may send users ads that claim to have scanned their

---

[4] Federal Trade Commission. (1999, August). Fair credit billing. In *Facts for consumers*. Retrieved June 22, 2011, from http://www.ftc.gov/bcp/edu/pubs/consumer/credit/cre16.shtm

[5] P2P Security. (2008, February). *OnGuard Online: Quick Facts*. Retrieved June 22, 2011, from http://www.onguardonline.gov/topics/p2p-security.aspx

[6] This is addressed in Chapter 20.

[7] P2P Security, supra.

computer and detected malware. The GetNetWise site can provide access to information about legitimate security vendors.[8]

- Antivirus software protects computers from viruses that can destroy computer data, slow a computer's performance, cause a crash, or even allow spammers to send e-mail to other computers. Antivirus software works by scanning the computer and incoming e-mail for viruses, and then deleting them.
- Spyware software monitors or controls computer use. It can send pop-up ads, redirect computer to websites, monitor Internet surfing, or record keystrokes, which can lead to the theft of personal information.
- A firewall helps keep hackers from using a computer to send out personal information without permission. A firewall prevents outside attempts to access the computer.

Spammers search the Internet for unprotected computers they can control and use anonymously to send spam. They turn these computers into a robot network, known as a *botnet*. A botnet can be made up of many thousands of home computers that are remotely directed to send out spam e-mails.

Malware can be hidden in free, downloadable software applications like games, file-sharing programs, customized toolbars, and the like. Malware can also come through an e-mail with attachments, links, or photos that, when opened, install hidden software.

Hackers can also gain access to a computer through security flaws in web browsers and operating-system software that don't have the latest security updates. Browser and operating-system companies regularly issue security patches for flaws that are found in their systems. This is why it is important that computers provide updating alerts and that students regularly download and install these security patches.

PASSWORDS

Another important security measure is to use safe and effective passwords. Hackers have various methods they use to try to figure out passwords. Teach students to use passwords that have at least eight characters, including numbers or symbols. One way to create a password is to use a sentence that contains the words that can be turned into numbers and use the first letters of the words. For example, "I would like to meet you for lunch" becomes the password "Iwl2my4l."

Passwords should not be shared with others. Many times teens will share their passwords with friends, including those with whom they have

---

[8] http://www.getnetwise.org/

a personal relationship. They must understand that friends don't ask friends for passwords.

BACKUPS

Students should know the importance of regularly backing up the files on their computer onto an external hard drive. This will help protect their files in the event of a security breach, theft, or accident that causes some damage to their computer.

DETECTING AND RESPONDING TO SECURITY PROBLEMS

Signs that a computer is infected with malware are that it slows down, malfunctions, displays repeated error messages, serves up many pop-up ads, displays web pages that were not selected, or similar actions.

If a computer is acting in this manner, it is very important to stop shopping, banking, and any other online activities that involve user names, passwords, or sending other sensitive information.

User steps include confirming that the security software is up to date, using the software to scan the computer, and deleting anything that is of concern. If this does not appear to resolve the problem, it is time to seek professional help.

SCAMS

Many scams seek the disclosure of financial identity information or are efforts to trick the person into doing something that will allow an invasion of their computer security, generally also for the purpose of identity theft. There are also many other kinds of scams. The FTC provides complete information on many different kinds of scams.[9] The scams students might most often fall into include work at home and college scholarship scams.

INSTRUCTIONAL APPROACH

The issues of identity theft, computer security, and scams are not as closely related to social norms as other issues. Therefore, these issues can be taught in a more direct instruction manner. Generally, these lessons are most appropriate at the high school level.

---

[9] Avoiding scams. (2008, February). *OnGuard Online: Quick facts*. Retrieved June 22, 2011, from http://www.onguardonline.gov/topics/avoiding-scams.aspx; Email scams. (2008, February). *OnGuard Online: Quick facts*. Retrieved June 22, 2011, from http://www.onguardonline.gov/topics/email-scams.aspx

In addition to the FTC materials, an excellent resource for information about how to prevent identity theft comes from the National Crime Prevention Council. *Protecting Teens From Identity Theft: A Guide for Adults* is a helpful document that could be sent home to parents.[10] *Teens: Protecting Your Identity From Thieves* is an excellent document for students.[11]

A creative instructional strategy would be to have the students review materials related to computer security on a variety of sites and then create their own computer-security checklist. The class, as a group, could finalize this checklist. The students could then use this checklist to assess the security of their home computer. An alternative would be to encourage them offer to do a computer security check with a neighbor or an adult friend.

Likely one of the best sources of "teachable moments" materials addressing scams is your spam digest or your student's spam digests. A possible instructional activity would be a "scam scavenger hunt." Have the students search for materials that are either a scam or news articles that describe these kinds of scams.

INSTRUCTIONAL OBJECTIVES

- (Grades 4–5) Students will describe the actions necessary to ensure effective computer security and will ask parent approval before registering on sites.
- (Grades 6–12) Students will describe the actions necessary to ensure effective computer security.
- (Grades 6–12) Students will recognize indicators of a scam, including offers that are too good to be true and threats that if they do not disclose personal information, something bad will happen to their account.

---

[10] National Crime Prevention Council. (n.d.). *Protecting teens from identity theft: A guide for adults.* Retrieved June 22, 2011, from http://www.ncpc.org/programs/teens-crime-and-the-community/publications-1/preventing-theft/adult_teen%20id%20theft.pdf

[11] National Crime Prevention Council. (n.d.). *Teens: Protecting your identity from thieves.* Retrieved June 22, 2011, from http://www.ncpc.org/programs/teens-crime-and-the-community/publications-1/preventing-theft/contact

Abide by the Terms

Act in Accord With Policies, Terms, and Laws

Responsible decision making starts with a recognition that there are common values and standards that apply to actions using digital technologies. Groups of people naturally develop a set of accepted behaviors that governs the ways in which they are expected to interact with each other. Without a set of common standards, there would be increased contention.

Due to the factors discussed in Chapter 2 that relate to what is commonly known as *online disinhibition*, some users of digital technologies have the perception that there are no or fewer standards. There certainly is not the kind of centralized government control that is evident in other social institutions. But there are certainly many sources of "rules" for use of digital technologies. These include policies, terms of use agreements, criminal laws, and civil torts. The common thread of these rules is the need to avoid harm to others or the integrity of the system.

POLICIES

Internet use policies generally address issues such as the intended purpose of the system, permitted activities, disallowed activities, and provisions governing when and how an individual's activities might be monitored or investigated.

The policies that all students are likely aware of are the district's Internet and cell-phone use policies. If they go to a college or university, these institutions also have policies for the use of the Internet through the university system. When they take a job where there is the possibility of accessing the Internet as part of their job responsibilities, their employer will also have a policy governing this use.

A key issue that must be discussed related to these policies is the intended purpose. School districts and employers are not providing students with Internet use to support their socializing, game playing, and other personal enjoyment activities. These are *limited purpose* systems, as compared to students' off-campus Internet activities. It is very important to make this distinction clear to students while they are at school. This is in preparation for their success while in the workplace. Employers have a dim view of employees who waste time and technological resources to play around online.

Cell-phone policies for K–12 schools address the allowed use of the phones while students are on campus, as well as provisions governing when school officials can review private records. Students should know that school officials can generally view their private records only if they have a reasonable suspicion that the cell phone has been used in a manner that is contrary to policy or the law. However, the extent of review must be limited to the suspicion. If students have any questions, they should be sure to tell a school official that they want their parents to be present before any records on their cell phone are viewed.

TERMS OF USE

Interactive websites, where users are allowed to communicate and to post material, have terms of use agreements. So do cell-phone companies. These terms of use also describe the actions that are permitted and disallowed when using the site or service. Common provisions address security, copyright infringement, and harmful actions, including illegal actions.

It is helpful for students to know the provisions of the terms of use agreements, both to guide their own decisions and to know when the behavior of others has violated these terms. In either event, an abuse report could be filed.

CRIMINAL LAWS

States have rewritten their criminal laws related to harmful communications to incorporate digital communications. An excellent source of information on common laws is a page on the site of the National Conference of State Legislatures. The following helpful information is from their website.

Cyberstalking. Cyberstalking is the use of the Internet, email or other electronic communications to stalk, and generally refers to a pattern of threatening or malicious behaviors. Cyberstalking may be considered the most dangerous of the three types of Internet harassment, based on a posing credible threat of harm. Sanctions range from misdemeanors to felonies.

Cyberharassment. Cyberharassment differs from cyberstalking in that it is generally defined as not involving a credible threat. Cyberharassment usually pertains to threatening or harassing email messages, instant messages, or to blog entries or websites dedicated solely to tormenting an individual. Some states approach cyberharrassment by including language addressing electronic communications in general harassment statutes, while others have created stand-alone cyberharassment statutes.[1]

The criminal statutes that could also apply to acts conducted online or while using a cell phone include the following:

- *Invasion of personal privacy.* This includes taking a photo in a place where privacy is expected.
- *Hate crimes.* Criminal acts accomplished using digital technologies that are motivated by bias because a person is a member of a certain social group.
- *Child pornography.* Creating, possessing, or distributing photos of minors that depict explicit sexual conduct.
- *Sexual exploitation.* If an older teen seeks a sexual relationship with a younger teen, this could be considered sexual exploitation. The age at which young people can consent to sex varies in the different states. There are generally "safe harbor" provisions that will not result in conviction of like-age peers. The provisions vary by state.
- *Threats.* The declaration of an intent to inflict harm on a person or that person's property.
- *Sexting.* Some states are now enacting laws related to sexting—sending nude photos of minors. This is being done in an attempt to have lower criminal consequences for what is recognized as teen behavior that may fit the statutory definition of child pornography, but is not the same thing.

[1] National Conference of State Legislatures. (2011, January). Cyberstalking, cyberharassment, and cyberbullying laws. Retrieved June 22, 2011, from http://www.ncsl.org/default.aspx?tabid=13495

CIVIL LAWS

The civil law legal theories are considered *intentional torts*. Intentional torts are offenses that are committed by a person who intends to do an act that results in causing harm—essentially, an intentional wrongdoing.

In civil litigation, the injured person can request financial damages from the person who has caused harm. In cases where the person is a minor, the case is filed against the parents or legal guardians. The financial damages can include loss due to pain and suffering, costs of counseling, losses related to lowered school performance or school avoidance, and the like. The injured person can also request an injunction, which is a court order requiring certain behavior or the cessation of certain behavior.

These intentional torts can apply in situations where a student might post very harmful material about another person. In these situations, the claims would be filed against the parents of the child under state laws that allow parents to be sued for the intentional torts committed by their child or under a parental negligence theory. The intentional torts include the following:

- *Defamation (or libel).*[2] The cause of action of defamation (or libel) is based on the publication of a false and damaging statement. The statement must identify the target and the statement must harm the target's reputation in the community. It must also be demonstrated that the person committing the defamation intentionally published the statement or failed to prevent its publication when he or she should have acted to prevent such publication. The defense to a claim based on defamation is that the statement is true.

- *Invasion of privacy: Publicity given to private life.*[3] An invasion of privacy claim involves the public disclosure of private facts. Public disclosure of private facts occurs when a person publicly discloses a nonpublic detail of another person's private life, when the effect would be highly offensive to a reasonable person. Defenses to actions based on invasion of privacy are that the facts are "newsworthy" or that the target gave consent. Activities of young people that are the subject of Internet denigration are unlikely to be newsworthy. Consent must be provided by someone who is considered capable of giving legal consent. Minors are not considered capable of giving legal consent.

---

[2] Restatement (Second) of Torts § 558 (1977).
[3] Restatement (Second) of Torts § 652D (1977).

- *Invasion of privacy: False light.*[4] The claim of false light can be made when there has been a publication that was made with actual malice that placed an individual in a false light that would be highly offensive or embarrassing to reasonable persons. Creating and publishing a photo that superimposes a person's head onto a nude photo would fall under a claim of false light.

- *Intentional infliction of emotional distress.*[5] The claim of intentional infliction of emotional distress supports a legal action when a person's intentional or reckless actions are outrageous and intolerable and have caused extreme distress. To support this claim, actions must be considered to be very outrageous and regarded as utterly intolerable in a civilized community. Unfortunately, many of the more egregious incidents of cyberbullying would appear to meet this standard.

INSTRUCTIONAL APPROACHES

A review of the school's Internet use policy, which frequently occurs with students at the beginning of the school year, presents the opportunity for a larger discussion about the values and standards incorporated into the policy. Students can also bring in a copy of the terms of use agreements of their favorite websites. For Grades 9–12, students could be provided with examples of use policies from local employers and government agencies. Have the students compare and contrast the provisions, especially noting the similarities. Compare these standards to the guidelines for actions that the student's parents have expressed. Discuss the reasons for the similarities.

Have the students work as teams to outline what terms they would recommend be included in a school, site, or employer policy. This would provide the opportunity for them to "switch hats" from being the ones controlled under such agreements to thinking about the values and standards they would want these agreements to contain—and why.

The involvement of law enforcement officials in the discussion of the criminal laws, which will allow the presentation of information about specific state laws, is highly advisable. The discussion should explain how law enforcement officials can use the material posted by people online to support convictions, how they are able to identify people by filing a search warrant with the sites or services, as well as common investigation methods, such as searching for evidence of trafficking child pornography

---

[4] Restatement (Second) of Torts § 652E (1977).
[5] Restatement (Second) of Torts § 46 (1977).

through P2P networking services. Providing news stories that illustrate actual arrests of teens will also be helpful in getting the message across about these more serious behaviors. News stories of situations where someone has filed a lawsuit for personal damages can provide a helpful resource for class discussion.

INSTRUCTIONAL OBJECTIVES

- (Grades 4–12) Students will describe the common provisions of school and employee Internet use agreements and terms of use agreements for social networking and other sites and services. Students will explain that the purposes for such provisions are to prevent harmful consequences to others or to the site or service and will recognize that the consequences for violating such terms generally involve restrictions on use or other consequences.
- (Grades 4–12) Students will distinguish the difference between online socializing and the use of technology resources for educational and (Grades 6–12) for employment purposes.
- (Grades 4–12) Students will demonstrate the ability to guide their online activities while at school in accord with provisions of the district's Internet use including the educational use restriction.
- (Grades 8–12) Students will describe the criminal laws that could apply to activities using digital technologies and explain the harm that these laws seek to prevent.
- (Grades 8–12) Students will describe the ways in which a teen and his or her parents could be sued for financial damages in the event that the teen engaged in behavior using digital technologies that caused harm to another.

16

Stay Out of the Garbage

Avoid Objectionable and Illegal Material

In a 2005 survey, the Crimes Against Children Research Center (CACRC) found that 13 percent of young Internet users aged ten through seventeen had visited X-rated websites on purpose in the past year.[1] Even more youth—34 percent—were exposed to online pornography they did not want to see. However, almost three quarters of all exposure incidents (74 percent) were not at all or only a little upsetting to youth, thus it is important not to overemphasize the potential harm.

ACCIDENTAL ACCESS

Based on the survey results, accidental access occurred in this manner:

> Most incidents happened while youth were surfing the web (83%). More than one-third of surfing exposure incidents happened when youth were doing online searches (40%). Clicking on links in other web sites led to 17% of exposures. Misspelled web addresses led to 12%, and 14% were from pop-up ads. In 13% of surfing incidents the exposure happened in various other ways, and in 4% of incidents youth did not know how the exposure happened.[2]

When asked in open-ended questions about such access, some of the young people seemed to place the blame for such access on their own lack

---

[1] Wolak, J., Mitchell, K. J., and Finkelhor, D. (2007, February). Unwanted and wanted exposure to online pornography in a national sample of youth Internet users. *Pediatrics, 119*(2), 247–257. Retrieved June 22, 2011, from http://www.unh.edu/ccrc/pdf/CV153.pdf

[2] Wolak et al. (2006), supra, p. 36.

of attentiveness. Others did indicate their understanding that sites that host this kind of material use tricks that will lead to accidental access.

Young people appear to have good skills in responding. The great majority of youth (92 percent) simply removed themselves from the situation by blocking or leaving the site or computer. In more than half of incidents (52 percent), youth did not tell anyone about the incidents. When youth did tell someone, it was usually a parent or guardian. When asked why they did not tell anyone, 75 percent said the incidents were not serious enough, 12 percent said they were afraid to, and 9 percent said they thought they might get in trouble.

The overreliance on filtering appears to have resulted in false security and the failure to teach students how to avoid accidental access and effectively respond. Most of the ways in which these teens accidentally accessed pornography could have been prevented with safe surfing strategies.

Accidental access can be reduced by effective technical prevention and safe searching strategies. The possible emotional harm can be reduced by making sure every student knows exactly what to do if something bad comes on the screen and is warned in advance about the potential of "mousetrapping"—getting trapped on a site with pornographic material.

INTENTIONAL ACCESS

As noted, the CACRC researchers also asked about intentional access. As could be expected, the majority of the young people who intentionally accessed online pornography were teen boys. The rates of access increased with age. More than a third of sixteen- and seventeen-year-old males had intentionally accessed these sites. This was not considered surprising, as this kind of behavior is associated with the high degree of sexual interest that is natural within this age group. Use of file-sharing programs to download pornography was frequent. Of particular note is that the researchers found some association between youth who were intentionally accessing pornography and measures of depression and rule breaking. The researchers noted,

> It is also important not to overstate associations between wanted exposure and delinquency or depression. Sexual curiosity among teenage boys is normal, and many might say that visiting X-rated Web sites is developmentally appropriate behavior. However, some researchers have expressed concern that exposure to online pornography during adolescence may lead to a variety of negative consequences, including undermining of accepted social values

and attitudes about sexual behavior, earlier and promiscuous sexual activity, sexual deviancy, sexual offending, and sexually compulsive behavior.

It is by no means established that online pornography acts as a trigger for any of these problems in youth or adult viewers. However, if it can promote deviant sexual interests or offending among some youth viewers, then the subgroup of youth Internet users with delinquent tendencies could include the youth most vulnerable to such effects, given the association between juvenile sexual offending and antisocial behavior. Also, some researchers have found relationships between depression and online sexually compulsive behavior. This suggests that the group of depressed youth Internet users could contain some who might be at risk for developing online sexual compulsions, which could interfere with normal sexual development or impair their ability to meet daily obligations and to develop healthy relationships with peers.[3]

This may be an issue to address in a sex-education class. However, this discussion could be controversial and may not be considered appropriate in many communities. It is likely difficult, if not impossible, in many schools to make the following statement: "Many would say that visiting pornography sites is developmentally appropriate behavior for teens."

Here again, reliance on filtering is ridiculous. Any teen with minimal technical skills can easily bypass filtering software.

CHILD PORNOGRAPHY

It is exceptionally important to warn students about concerns associated with intentionally accessing child pornography. There are national and international initiatives directed at preventing the spread of child pornography. In the United States, the leading law enforcement initiative is called Innocent Images.[4] FBI agents and Internet Crimes Against Children law enforcement officers go online undercover into predicated locations using fictitious screen names. They engage in real-time chat or e-mail conversations with subjects to obtain evidence of criminal activity. They are also able to investigate the data streams to identify child pornography. They spend time in P2P networking environments. And many times they investigate or arrest teens and young adults.[5] A possible factor involved in

---

[3] Id., p. 9.

[4] http://www.fbi.gov/about-us/investigate/cyber/innocent/innocent

[5] Information conveyed to author by an investigator.

this is that it is possible that teen boys are much more interested in looking at nude photos of teen girls rather than adult women. They may not even know that looking at or collecting photos or minors is illegal.

Some of the negative-influence factors are at play here. Teens may well think that because these photos are easily available through P2P networking or on other sites, that it is perfectly appropriate for them to be looking at them. Also the fact that they feel invisible when doing this may influence inappropriate behavior. It is exceptionally important, especially in this area, that they know this is illegal and that criminal investigations are occurring, thus they can be identified and arrested, the consequences of which could potentially destroy their future.

Likely the teens who get heavily involved in this kind of trafficking are those who have other significant psychosocial problems. It is also possible that they become attracted to the groups of people involved in trafficking and feel emotionally supported by these individuals. They may even be groomed for participation, because they may be perceived by adult traffickers as having greater access to young people to obtain photos.

INSTRUCTIONAL ACTIVITIES

Teach students how to avoid accidental access. This is an issue that is not influenced by social norms and can be addressed through more direct instruction. The following are recommended safe surfing strategies:

- *Set it "safe."* Make sure your parents have installed security software, your browser blocks pop-ups, and your search engine is set to "safe search."
- *Read, think, then click.* Don't click on suspicious links.
- *Don't fall for traps.* Don't type URLs. This mistake could take you to a bad place. Type the name of the site in a search engine and then look carefully at the results before you click.
- *Delete the spam.* Don't open suspicious e-mail messages. Never click a link in an e-mail message unless you know the link is safe.
- *Turn it off and tell.* If "yucky stuff" appears on the screen, turn off the monitor, force quit the browser, or simply turn off the computer. Always tell a parent or a teacher that this happened so that the adult will know this was a mistake and you will not get into trouble. If this ever happens, someone should look at the computer and how the accident happened to make sure it won't happen again.

The issue of intentional access is a topic that is likely best addressed by a health teacher and a law enforcement officer. This instruction is best left to the high school level. Make sure to advise teens to talk with their friends about the dangers associated with access of digital images of nude children or teens. Clearly outline the legal consequences and the current law enforcement activities that could lead to detection and arrest.

Here are issues that should likely be addressed:

- What constitutes illegal pornography
- How the Internet, and especially the P2P networks, are heavily monitored by law enforcement
- The seriousness and legal implications of downloading and or trading of child pornography photos and videos
- Signs that a person's Internet usage, including access to pornography, is becoming addictive, and how and where someone could get help

INSTRUCTIONAL OBJECTIVES

- (Grades 4–12) Students will describe the techniques they can use to avoid accidentally accessing objectionable material and the actions they should take if such accidental access has occurred.
- (Grades 6–12) Students will understand that objectionable material often comes with malware.
- (Grades 9–12) Students will understand issues related to the creation, possession, and distribution of child pornography, including the laws against child pornography and the consequences of a conviction for violating those laws, as well as how law enforcement investigates these cases.

17

Don't Sell Yourself

Disclose and Consume Wisely

For major commercial companies, the Internet is a significant vehicle for market profiling and advertising. Young people are "hot prospects"— a highly targeted online demographic. Advertisers can track, trick, and target them largely outside of parent awareness. Companies know that the younger generation controls or influences billions of dollars of family purchasing decisions. Advertisers also know that it is possible to influence young people to make persistent pleas for items and make arguments to justify purchases.

During the teen years, brand loyalty—a preference for a specific brand of product or service—is established. Not only do marketers seek to influence young people's current spending and their influence on parental spending; they also want to influence future spending. Additionally, they want to raise the younger generation to think that it is perfectly natural to have websites know everything about them, so that these sites can direct advertising that is specifically targeted to their interests.

Advertisers have found the Internet to be an effective way to reach young people. Young people usually use the Internet alone, so advertisers can form a more direct relationship. Advertising online is less regulated than other forms of media.

There are many significant concerns associated with advertising to young people.[1] The advertisements negatively impact their social, emotional, and physical well-being. Advertisers may capitalize on the

---

[1] Wilcox, B. L., Kunkel, D., Cantor, J., Dowrick, P., Linn, S., & Palmer, E. (2004, February 20). *Report of the APA Taskforce on Advertising and Children*. American Psychological Association. Retrieved June 22, 2011, from http://www.apa.org/pi/families/resources/advertising-children.pdf

insecurities of youth by promoting the cool factor. Anyone who does not fit the advertiser's image of what is cool or who does not have their products or use their services may then be defined as a loser. Advertisers also promote highly sexualized photos of teens. The underlying message is that being skinny and sexy and having these cool products is necessary for popularity and happiness. There is also a significant relationship between advertising and obesity in children.

Our society appears to have accepted the idea of the provision of free or low-cost information or entertainment supported by advertising. If not for online advertising, the vast majority of commercial sites simply would not exist or would require payment of a subscription fee. Educate students about how profiling and advertising work so that they can be more aware of what is happening. This will hopefully enable them to recognize and avoid being manipulated by the profilers and advertisers and lead to greater personal control over their brand loyalty and purchasing decisions.

MARKET PROFILING

Profiling means the development of extensive database of demographic information and interest of users.[2] Profiles may include information provided online at various sites and it may be combined with information revealed on product registration or other surveys. Companies are also able to track Internet users as they visit different sites on the Internet and combine information about Internet use with the other database information.

The data are maintained in an aggregated manner that is tied to a persistent indicator, such as a user's profile or computer. These data are used to deliver advertisements for products or services that are most likely to be of interest to individual users, based the user's demographics and demonstrated interests and activities.

Many young people do not recognize when advertisers collect product-interest information from them. These are some of the strategies marketers use to get personal-contact and personal-interest information from young people:

- Registration forms or social networking profiles. These suggest that members provide information about their personal interests to be able to meet other young people with similar interests.
- Online contests, tests, quizzes, and "tell us what you think" surveys or other marketing surveys. Frequently, the site offers some

---

[2] Federal Trade Commission (2010, December 1). FTC staff issues privacy report, offers framework for consumers, businesses, and policymakers [Press release]. Retrieved June 22, 2011, from http://www.ftc.gov/opa/2010/12/privacyreport.shtm

kind of reward for completing these surveys, including bonus points, discount coupons, or a possibility of a reward.

- Registration on a site that results in placing a cookie on your computer. This cookie is necessary to reenter the site because it provides user registration information, but it is also used to track and transmit a significant amount of information about the computer, sites visited, links accessed, and the like.

A frequent statement of marketers is that people want them to know what they are interested in so they can receive ads that would be of interest. A study that investigated this found that

contrary to what many marketers claim, most adult Americans (66%) do not want marketers to tailor advertisements to their interests. Moreover, when Americans are informed of three common ways that marketers gather data about people in order to tailor ads, even higher percentages—between 73% and 86%—say they would not want such advertising.[3]

This study did not ask the respondents what they thought about websites engaging in behavioral advertising directed at their children. It is not hard to imagine what the response of parents would be.

ADVERTISING APPROACHES

Targeted or Behavioral Advertising

Using this market profile, the sites target advertisements to users, most frequently banner ads. The objective is to use the information they have to display ads for products and services that a user is more likely to be interested in, and thus more likely to click on. This, then, will generate income for the site.

Social Media Advertising

The latest hot Internet marketing idea builds on the idea of social norms: People are most likely to trust recommendations made by their friends regarding brands. Social network marketing leverages the power of the social connections that have been established on social networking

---

[3] Turow, J., King, J., Hoofnagle, C. J., Bleakley, A., & Hennessy, M. (2009, October 6). *Contrary to what marketers say, Americans reject tailored advertising and the three activities that enable it* (Departmental Papers [ASC]) [Abstract]. Retrieved June 22, 2011, from http://repository.upenn.edu/asc_papers/137/

sites and use these friendship connections to advertise. Here is how Facebook describes this in a FAQ:

> What does it mean to "Like" a Page or content off of Facebook?
> When you click "Like" on a Page, in an advertisement, or on content off of Facebook, you are making a connection. The connection will be displayed in your profile and on your Wall and your friends may receive a News Feed story about the connection. You may be displayed on the Page you connected to, in advertisements about that Page, or in social plugins next to the content you like. The Page may also post content into your News Feed or send you messages. You may also share this connection with applications on the Facebook Platform.[4]

In April 2010, Facebook and the Neilson Company published the joint report *Advertising Effectiveness: Understanding the Value of Social Media Impression.* As noted in a blog that announced this report,

> Study after study has shown that consumers trust their friends and peers more than anyone else when it comes to making a purchase decision. It's critical that we understand advertising not just in terms of "paid" media, but also in terms of how "earned" media (advertising that is passed along or shared among to friends and beyond) and social advocacy contribute to campaigns.
> This study of more than 800,000 Facebook users and ads from 14 brands in a variety of categories demonstrated that there was an increase in ad recall, awareness and purchase intent when the home-page ads on the social network mentioned friends of users who had become fans of the brand. Furthermore, the impact on awareness and recall was even greater when the ad appeared in a user's newsfeed indicting that the user's friend had become a fan of that brand.[5]

As will be discussed in the following chapter, this new approach of "social circle" advertising, which is grounded in having people send advertisements to their friends, is the underlying reason that sites encourage users to have many friends and why, as of the writing of this book, Facebook, the leading social networking site, refuses to establish default privacy settings for minors in a manner that will limit wide distribution.

---

[4] Retrieved June 22, 2011, from http://www.facebook.com/help/?faq=17115&ref_query=like

[5] Gibs, J. (2010, April 20). *Nielson/Facebook report: The value of social media ad impressions.* Retrieved June 22, 2011, from http://blog.nielsen.com/nielsenwire/online_mobile/nielsenfacebook-ad-report/

An interesting discussion with students would assess the degree to which they are interested in receiving advertisements from their friends through their social networking communications.

Search Return Advertisements

Whenever anyone conducts a search using a popular search engine, such as Google, Bing, or Yahoo, the very prominent links at the top and side of the search return are *search return advertisements* that are related to whatever topic they searched on.

Permission Marketing

Permission marketing is an opportunity offered to "opt in" to receive advertising. The theory behind permission marketing is that if a company asks permission to send advertising information to a person, and that person agrees, this provides the opportunity for the company to form a closer relationship with the person and to build brand loyalty. Many stores now ask if shoppers would like to provide them with their e-mail address and they then send advertisements via e-mail, frequently with coupons.

Advergaming

Advergaming is the integration of advertising messages into online games and activities. Instead of a thirty-second TV advertisement or a banner ad, advertisers can create conditions for young people to immerse themselves for extended periods of time interacting with advertising material in a gaming and activities environment. Advergaming initially started out as a vehicle on children's websites. Now many apps that are accessible through social networking sites are advergames.

PRIVACY ISSUES

"Do Not Track" Proposal

On December 1, 2010, the U.S. Federal Trade Commission (FTC) issued a preliminary staff report addressing the concerns of privacy, profiling, and advertising.[6] The report noted that industry efforts to address privacy through self-regulation have been too slow and have failed to provide adequate and meaningful protection. The report outlined the problems related to increasing advances in technology that allow for rapid data collection and sharing that are often invisible to consumers and

---

[6] Federal Trade Commission (2010, December 1), supra.

problems with lengthy, legalistic privacy policies that users usually don't read and don't understand if they do.

One key recommendation was the use of a simplified disclosure and choice system for users. This would involve a "do not track" mechanism governing the collection of information about user's Internet activity to deliver targeted advertisements and for other purposes that would involve the placement of a persistent setting on the consumer's browser signaling the user's choices about being tracked and receiving targeted ads. The FTC also indicates that it will provide expanded consumer education in this area. These materials will be very helpful for instructional activities.

Children's Online Privacy Protection Act

Under the Children's Online Privacy Protection Act (COPPA), websites must limit the information they can request from children under the age of thirteen.[7] COPPA restricts the kind of information children can post on these sites and requires a privacy policy and parental permission for registration. By age thirteen, young people are generally considered to be functioning like adults on general audience sites, such as social networking sites. By this age, there are generally no restrictions on the information that can be requested by the site or that the site encourages to be publicly posted.

There are questions about the effectiveness of COPPA in protecting the privacy of children, primarily because most parents do not understand the profiling practices and do not read or understand the privacy policies. Additionally, many children lie about their age to register on sites for users older than thirteen.

The FTC is conducting an assessment of COPPA, asking questions related to mobile technologies and other new technologies, the definition of *personal information*, methods to obtain parental consent, and the effectiveness of self-regulation by the sites.[8]

Privacy Policies

The following is an example of what a privacy policy for a teen site might say, along with a translation.[9] This privacy policy originally came

---

[7] http://www.ftc.gov/privacy/privacyinitiatives/childrens.html

[8] Federal Trade Commission. (2010, March 24). FTC seeks comment on children's online privacy protections; questions whether changes to technology warrant changes to agency rule [Press release]. Retrieved June 22, 2011, from http://www.ftc.gov/opa/2010/03/coppa.shtm

[9] http://www.quizrocket.com; Privacy Policy from October 2007, accessed through the Way Back Machine: http://web.archive.org/web/20071024125549/http://quizrocket.com/0/privacy/

from Quiz Rocket, a site with entertaining surveys where the questions are partially about the topic and partially about interests and activities. Quiz Rocket has since made their policy more unreadable. This earlier policy is used because it provides a clear statement of information to look for.

QuizRocket collects user information on certain portions of our Website, through methods which include, but are not limited to, responding to questions and surveys, registering for the site, or through various offers provided on site. *(Translation: We will collect anything you post that might help us determine what ads to show you. Note the "but not limited to" language. This is legalese indicating "and anything else we want to do.")*

The personal profile information you submit to QuizRocket and Advertisers remains your property, but by submitting that information to QuizRocket you grant QuizRocket the right to use that information for marketing purposes including, but not limited to, sharing such information via co-registration with Advertisers. *(Translation: Not only can we use your information for advertising, we can provide your information to any of our advertisers.)*

QuizRocket may also use such information to deliver certain direct marketing offers to you via telemarketing, e-mail marketing, direct mail, SMS messaging and other types of direct marketing, fulfill prizes, track compliance with our QuizRocket Rules, or for content improvement and feedback purposes. *(Translation: if you provide us with any other contact information, such as your address and phone number, you are also granting us permission to send you ads through these other methods.)*

We may sell the personal information that you supply to us to selected third parties. These businesses may include, but are not limited to: (a) providers of direct marketing services to via telemarketing, e-mail marketing, direct mail, SMS messaging and other types of direct marketing; and (b) providers of applications, including lookup and reference, data enhancement, suppression and validation. *(Translation: And we can provide your information, including contact information, to any other advertiser.)*

By agreeing to these terms, you hereby consent to disclosure of any record or communication to any third party when QuizRocket, in its sole discretion, determines the disclosure to be appropriate. *(Translation: No privacy.)*

POSITIVE USES OF THE INTERNET TO GUIDE WISE CONSUMPTION

The Internet can be used in a very effective manner to guide wise consumption. It can be a tool that facilitates prepurchasing investigations, purchasing, and postpurchase interactions.

It is possible to research products and companies very effectively online. A visit to a company website can provide insight into how well this company supports its products. Other sites or discussion groups may provide product reviews from satisfied or dissatisfied purchasers. Engaging in online prepurchasing investigations is essentially an activity that is grounded in assessing credibility.

It is also possible to form positive relationships with companies that have gained your loyalty and to receive discounts on purchases from these companies. This is the permission marketing approach discussed already. Signing up to receive e-mail advertising from a company you support will result in frequent or occasional coupons for discounts.

Purchasing can now be accomplished online. Online purchasing allows consumers to engage in price comparison and to purchase products that may not be easily available locally. When purchasing online, young people should carefully investigate the company and site to avoid providing financial information to a site that is not legitimate. These issues were addressed in Chapter 14.

Postpurchasing issues can also be addressed online. Can't find the user guide for a product your purchased? It will likely be available online. Need a replacement component? You can order it online. Companies also frequently have online troubleshooting FAQs. It is possible to send e-mail to the site to ask questions or seek guidance in addressing concerns. Some companies even have 24/7 chat help services.

Essentially, consumers either can be profiled and manipulated through targeted and social advertising or can gain significant power over their consumption decisions. The deciding factor on which direction young people will travel is grounded in their understanding of these issues. From this understanding will come power—and hopefully the incentive—to engage in responsible consumption.

INSTRUCTIONAL ACTIVITIES

The following are some issues that can be addressed in discussions with students:

- Discuss that the fact that advertising can be helpful in making us aware of certain products and services. But emphasize that it is always important to look carefully at the product or service and determine whether it is desirable and necessary—and not simply respond to the advertisers' techniques.

- Help students recognize the influence techniques that advertisers use. These might include the promotion of a product as being "cool" or something that is necessary in order to fit in with their peers. Ask students to find advertisement and describe the underlying influence technique that the advertiser is using in an effort to encourage their purchase.

- Ask students to review the material on their social networking profile and note what information may be of particular interest to advertisers. They should recognize that the information that Facebook or any other social networking site suggests they provide in their profile information is designed to provide information for advertisers.

- Encourage students to pay attention to the banner ads they are shown and try to figure out why the site thinks that they would be more likely to click on a particular ad. Ask them to find the ads that are directly related to some piece of information they have posted on their site as an interest or activity.

The FTC has an useful site called Admongo that provides excellent instructional activities related to the underlying issues of advertising and consumption.[10]

A helpful instructional activity, especially at the high school level, is to have students bring in a copy of the privacy policy for site they use, such as an app site, and then look through the policy to answer the following questions:

- What information is collected?
- How is that information used?
- Does the site provide the user's information to others?
- Is there any way to "opt out" of this profile information collection?

An excellent resource for high school students is found on the Facebook website: Under a link at the bottom of the page "Advertising," students can find a significant amount of information on how companies can advertise on Facebook.[11]

Focus students' attention on how to use the Internet to engage in wise consumption. Discuss what they might look for in prepurchasing

---

[10] http://www.admongo.gov/

[11] http://www.facebook.com/advertising/

investigations, the issues they might want to consider in agreeing to a permission marketing arrangement, issues around safe online purchasing, and how to effectively use commercial sites to address and resolve postpurchasing issues.

INSTRUCTIONAL OBJECTIVES

- (Grades 4–12) Students will recognize that most of the sites they visit are supported through advertising revenues and that this will lead to efforts to create a market profile of their demographics and interests that will be used to direct specific advertisements to them.
- (Grades 4–12) Students will describe the various forms of advertising online, including banner ads, advergaming, permission marketing, and viral marketing.
- (Grades 4–5) Students will know to ask a parent before providing personal contact information or responding to a quiz or game that asks them about personal interests.
- (Grades 6–12) Students will identify the specific techniques used online to obtain their demographic and interest data and recognize that much of what they post online will be maintained in an aggregated manner to support targeted advertising.
- (Grades 6–12) Students will develop personal standards regarding the amount and kinds of personal information they will provide when such information is specifically solicited or when they have the opportunity to control the collection of such information.
- (Grades 9–12) Students will develop effective standards to follow in engaging in prepurchasing investigations, agreeing to permission marketing arrangements, purchasing safely online, and effectively engaging in postpurchase interactions.

18 Protect Your Face and Friends

Be Savvy and Civil When Networking

Social networking sites allow teens to create personal profiles, post photos and writings, and connect with friends. Many teens, as well as adults, are very active in social networking. At this point in time, when the discussion is social networking, the site that is most often involved is Facebook.[1] However, Google recently announced its new social network called Google Plus or Google+. Other less well known social networking sites have been established for children and tweens. This chapter will address issues that relate to the use of any social networking site. However, because of its popularity, there will be a specific focus on Facebook.

The Cyber Savvy survey on http://embracingdigitalyouth.org has many questions that focus on social networking practices and the rationale for these practices. This survey will demonstrate that the majority of students, especially those who are older, have a good understanding of these issues, engage or intend to engage in safe practices, and have a good understanding of the reasons for those safe practices. This survey insight can be very helpful in influencing younger students or those students who have not thought these issues through thoroughly.

The common features of a social networking site include the following:[2]

- *Personal profile.* This allows users to present information about themselves. This generally includes a section where the site suggests the kinds of information that users ought to share, including

---

[1] http://www.facebook.com

[2] Because Facebook is the site that most teens currently use, Facebook's terms are used in this chapter.

photo, birth date, interests, relationship interests, bio, school or work affiliations, and the like. The profile information is generally relatively static.

- *Establishing friendships.* Once a user has established a profile, that user can then send "friend requests" to other users. When a friend link has been established, each user's profile photo shows up on the other user's profile. Depending on the privacy settings, friends generally have a greater ability to access information on their friends' profiles and communicate.
- *Public communications and information sharing.* A place where the user can post information and friends can post comments or indicate that they like this material.
- *Photos and videos.* Users can post photos or videos which others can comments on.
- *Private messages.* The ability to send private messages to friends or others on the site.
- *Real-time communications.* The social networking version of instant messaging.
- *Apps (short for "applications") and games.* Software application programs that are on other sites and are accessed through a social networking site. Apps and games are generally used for entertainment purposes.
- *Mobile access.* The ability to access by using a cell phone
- *Information sharing.* Google+ allows people to easily gather online information they are interested in and then share that information with a select circle.

For students, the risks associated with social networking include many of the risks that are discussed in this book:

- Failure to set the privacy settings in a manner that will limit access of their personal information to only those people who they have "friended"
- Posting material that could negatively affect their reputation or attract unsafe people—or that others could use against them
- Posting material that could negatively damage the reputation of someone else or could cause others harm or place them at risk
- Being emotionally harmed when other people post hurtful or damaging information or photos or send hurtful messages
- Connecting with unsafe people, who are able to effectively "image manage" in this environment and can find information about a young person's interests and activities that can be used to form a relationship

- Publicly sharing information that can be used for identity theft, such as their accurate birth date and hometown, which can be used to find their social security number
- Publicly sharing information that could lead to other harm, such as posting a report that they will be out of town when their address is also provided or is easily found, thus resulting in home theft
- Publicly sharing their cell phone number, which could then be used by people who send them hurtful messages or for sending unwanted advertisements
- Failure to control how the sites, as well as app, game, and other partner sites, obtain a massive amount of personal information that is being used for product promotion

TERMS OF USE AND ABUSE REPORTING

Use of social networking sites is governed by terms of use. These terms prohibit actions that could cause harm to others or to the site. Most students have not likely read the terms. Making an assignment to read the terms of use would likely be a helpful exercise. Key abuse provisions of Facebook's Statement of Rights and Responsibilities are as follows:[3]

- You will not bully, intimidate, or harass any user.
- You will not post content that is hateful, threatening, or porno-graphic; incites violence; or contains nudity or graphic or gratu-itous violence.
- You will not use Facebook to do anything unlawful, misleading, malicious, or discriminatory.

Other sites have similar terms that restrict similar kinds of irrespon-sible or hurtful activities. All social networking sites have procedures to report abuse, which is a violation of the terms. When abuse is reported, the reports are reviewed by staff of the site. This review can take some time, so a response may not be immediate. Also, sometimes, what a user may consider abuse does not meet the standards set forth in the terms of use or the guidelines of the site. Students must always have a backup plan if the site does not respond promptly or if the site refuses to resolve the abuse in the manner desired by the user. The site's help features generally provide helpful information on how to file an abuse report.

As of the writing of this book, Facebook is developing an approach that will allow for expedited handling of abuse reports by authorized

---

[3] http://www.facebook.com/terms.php?ref=pf

school officials. This should help to rapidly address abusive situations that are impacting the school community.

PRIVACY SETTINGS

Necessary Understanding About the Social Networking Business Model

The financial engine that is fueling these social networking sites is market profiling and advertising. The CEO of Facebook, Mark Zuckerberg, recently noted his perception that the protection of personal privacy is no longer a "social norm."[4] Is the protection of privacy no longer a social norm, or does Facebook want people to think privacy is no longer the norm, because massive public disclosure supports their advertising income? Because of this business model, the driving motivation of social networking sites is to encourage its users to

- publicly share lots of information about themselves, as well as their friends—this information goes into each user's market profile; and
- establish many friendship links, which are used to support social media advertising strategies that were discussed in the prior chapter.[5]

Both of these activities can lead to greater risk. It is essential that student understand why sites encourage extensive postings and friending, and the importance of making smart choices.

Privacy Settings and Zuckering

Facebook's current approach for privacy settings is to establish the default settings for minors, to provide for significant public disclosure. Facebook does provide a way for users to reset the privacy settings to better limit access to their personal profile, but it is necessary for users to find and change many settings to achieve a sufficient level of privacy protection.

The failure to establish default settings for minors to be as safe as possible is especially concerning. Because of their lack of sophistication, young people may not be sufficiently attentive to the potential risks. In a research study of college students and Facebook Privacy Settings, the researchers found that college students who were less technically sophisticated were not as active in changing their privacy settings.

---

[4] Facebook's Zuckerberg says privacy no longer a "social norm" (VIDEO). (2010, January 11). *Huffington Post.* Retrieved June 20, 2011, from http://www.huffingtonpost.com/2010/01/11/facebooks-zuckerberg-the_n_417969.html

[5] Such as those that were described in Chapter 17.

The relationship between adjusting privacy settings and frequency of use as well as skill suggests that technological familiarity matters when it comes to how people approach the privacy settings of their Facebook accounts. This is particularly significant when we consider the role of default settings. If those who are the least familiar with a service are the least likely to adjust how their account is set up regarding privacy matters then they are the most likely to be exposed if the default settings are open or if the defaults change in ways that expose more of their content. This suggests that the vulnerability of the least skilled population is magnified by how companies choose to set or adjust default privacy settings.[6]

Given that the researchers were investigating the concerns associated with college users, clearly the concerns associated with the ability of teens, or tweens, to competently change the privacy settings to a safer level are even more significant. Additionally, given that tweens and teens lack the brain development and developmental experiences of college students, there are greater concerns related to the potential harms associated with their social networking activities.

Concerns about the default settings for minors on all social networking sites are an issue that is being aggressively considered by the European Commission. In a report released on June 21, 2011, Neelie Kroes, the commission's head of digital affairs, stated:

I am disappointed that most social networking sites are failing to ensure that minors' profiles are accessible only to their approved contacts by default. I will be urging them to make a clear commitment to remedy this in a revised version of the self-regulatory framework we are currently discussing. This is not only to protect minors from unwanted contacts but also to protect their online reputation. Youngsters do not fully understand the consequences of disclosing too much of their personal lives online. Education and parental guidance are necessary, but we need to back these up with protection until youngsters can make decisions based on full awareness of the consequences.[7]

---

[6] Boyd, D., & Hargittai, E. (2010, August) Facebook privacy settings: Who cares? *First Monday, 5*(8). Retrieved June 20, 2011, from http://firstmonday.org/htbin/cgiwrap/bin/ojs/index.php/fm/article/view/3086/2589

[7] European Commission. (2011, June 21). Digital agenda: Only two social networking sites protect privacy of minors' profiles by default [Press release]. Retrieved June 22, 2011, from http://europa.eu/rapid/pressReleasesAction.do?reference=IP/11/762&format=HTML&aged=0&language=EN&guiLanguage=en

Hopefully, at some point in time, Facebook, as well as all other social networking sites, will demonstrate a more responsible approach to the concerns associated with their default privacy settings. Unfortunately, at this point in time, social media advertising objectives appear to have a higher priority than youth safety.

INSTRUCTIONAL CONCERNS

There are a number of concerns associated with providing instruction that specifically relates to social networking.

Underage Users

Under the Children's Online Privacy Protection Act, which was discussed in Chapter 17, the minimum age for young people to register on the most popular sites, including Facebook, is thirteen. Clearly, there are many students in elementary school who have a Facebook presence—generally with the approval of their parents. By middle school, the majority of students are on Facebook. There are social networking environments that have been established for younger children that have greater safety features. A very excellent list of social networking sites for kids and tweens has been provided by Common Sense Media.[8] Unfortunately, these sites do not appear to be as popular.

So, on the one hand, it is important to talk about social networking safety with children and tweens. But on the other, talking about social networking safety could appear to legitimize being on Facebook and could lead students who are not to think they are being left behind.

There are some possible ways to handle this.

- Simply provide specific instruction related to use of Facebook or any other site and indicate that deciding when they should join should be a decision they make with their parents. This is likely the best approach in middle school.
- Discuss issues of social networking safety in the context of sites that have been approved for young people under the age of thirteen. This is likely an appropriate approach for fourth- and fifth-grade students and may also work in sixth and seventh grade.
- Strive to address the concerns in the context of the discussions around posting information and connecting with people—and

---

[8] Social networking for kids. (n.d.). *Common Sense Media*. Retrieved June 22, 2011, from http://www.commonsensemedia.org/website-lists/social-networking-kids?utm_source=newsletter06.23.11&utm_medium=email&utm_campaign=feature2

just "slip in" the discussions around social networking sites. The problem with this latter approach is that an important discussion that will be left out is the exceptionally important concerns associated with the privacy settings.

Instruction on Privacy Settings and Practices

Clearly, students should make changes to Facebook's default privacy settings. But teachers should not be expected to take the amount of time that would be necessary to gain expertise in these settings and then specifically teach students how to change the settings. Furthermore, it is not possible to provide specific instruction on settings in this book because these may change.

Because of these limitations, the guidance provided in this chapter is more general in nature. The focus is on strategies that can be applied in any social networking environment to remain safe, protect your reputation, respect others, and demonstrate responsibility for the well-being of others.

CORE CONCEPTS AND INSTRUCTIONAL APPROACHES

Protect Your Personal Privacy

- Make sure your privacy settings and practices are safe and wise.
  - Choosing the "friends" setting is the safest choice. Otherwise, disable, deselect, or disallow sharing of information. If any setting indicates "public," this likely should be changed.
  - Go thoroughly through all privacy settings—accessing every link on the Privacy Settings page to go down into the different pages of settings. Look for additional privacy settings that are associated with specific features. If in doubt, do a search on the "(site name) (name of feature or setting), privacy" to find out more, or ask a parent or an older teen for assistance.
  - Whenever a new feature is announced, review the announcement and any new settings to ensure privacy is protected.
- Suggested activities:
  - Have the students research the privacy settings on the other social networking sites for kids, teens, and tweens. Have students prepare and illustrate their own set of ten privacy-protection tips.
  - Encourage students to evaluate the differences between various social networking sites in terms of perspectives on personal privacy. This analysis can help them develop greater sensitivity to the larger issues of the protection of privacy online and how different companies approach these issues with different philosophies.

○ Discuss social media advertising. Watch for news articles about this form of advertising. Help students understand how the encouragement to post lots of information which is shared widely is related to these advertising objectives.

Protect Your Face (Reprise of "Think Before You Post")

- Remember that "friends only" does not mean "private."
  ○ Suggest to students that they consider who else might be able to review their profile if a friend shares such access.
- Present yourself as your best.
  ○ A social networking profile provides the opportunity to present the best aspects of who you are. Students should be encouraged to reflect carefully on what they want their public image to be.
- Just because a social networking site suggests that users provide certain personal information does not mean that it is safe or wise to provide it.
  ○ The information social networking sites may suggest users provide, such as interests and activities, relationship interests, telephone, address, and the like, is all used for market profiling. If students are just connecting with friends, there is no reason to provide much, if any, of this information.
  ○ Providing some information could present risk. Describing relationship interests could attract unwanted attention. Providing an address could lead to home theft, especially if they also post that they are out of town. Providing a cell number could lead to unwanted advertising sent to their cell phone or contact from people who are not safe.
- Use a profile photo that presents a positive image.
  ○ Students must recognize that their profile photo will appear on the profiles of all of their friends, and on any profile or page where they comment or indicate that they like. It will also appear randomly on other people's profiles with a suggestion that this person should friend them.
  ○ There is likely a direct relationship between the degree to which they appear provocative and the number of messages or friendship requests they will receive from people with whom they likely should not associate.
- Suggested activities:
  ○ Encourage students to write statements that reflect their personal standards for how they will present themselves in their personal profiles. Have them share these statements as posters or through a presentation.

○ Have the students list the kinds of information they are encouraged to provide on a social networking site, describe how this information might be used, identify the potential risks associated with providing different kinds information, and make recommendations on what kind of information to provide and how. Encourage the students to think of words that they would suggest provide the basis for determining what kind of picture would be appropriate or inappropriate for a profile photo. One feature on social networking sites that can be used in a way that can help to establish a positive image is the bio feature. Have students work on a bio statement that reflects the person they are and how they want others to see them.

○ Encourage students to review profiles of other teens or adults and describe, without naming names, material posted that they perceive does not reflect well on these teens or adults.

Protect Yourself and Your Circle of Friends (Reprise of Connect Safely)

• Be careful about whom you friend and what friendship groups or circles you establish.

○ Especially when students are younger, they should only friend people they know in person—or possibly someone whom a trusted friend knows in person. If they fail to follow this rule, they could establish a link with someone who may be deceptive and possibly dangerous.

○ It is also important to consider the safety of their friends. By friending someone unknown, they could provide this person with access to postings made by their friends.

○ Make sure students understand the reason social networking sites want them to have many friends is so that they might share product interests with their friends.

○ Young people with greater social anxiety may think that having many friends equates to higher social status. Encourage students to focus on the quality of their social networking friends, not quantity.

○ On Facebook, it is possible to establish *groups*. Google+ has a strong focus on establishing *circles*. This requires thinking about the different kinds of friends we might have. For example, teens may establish one group or circle for family members, another for a specific extracurricular organization they are a part of, another for close friends, and yet another for their wider circle of friends.

- Suggested activity:
  - One thinking activity is to encourage students to outline their personal standards for making a decision on whether to accept or send a friendship request. Suggest that they consider the character and behavior standards of people whom they want to be able to have access to their personal information and news about their lives. They should be specifically encouraged to consider standards in situations where they do not know this person in real life. Then expand the discussion into different types of friends. Encourage them to think of personal standards that relate to what kinds of information they might share with different kinds of friends.

Report Abuse of Yourself or Others

- If someone abuses you or another person, report this to the social networking site.
  - The easiest way to report abuse is in the "Report" button that is located on pages throughout the site. Address what to do if abuse is reported and the site does nothing in response— because this could happen. When it does, the person who is being abused may feel helpless. It is exceptionally important for students to know that a backup plan is absolutely necessary.
- Suggested activity:
  - Many youth have seen, and hopefully reported, abuse. The discussion on reporting abuse should focus very strongly on the role of witnesses to abuse, and the importance of such reports.

Respect the Privacy of Your Friends—Make a Pact

- Do not disclose personal information or photos of a friend without that person's explicit consent.
  - It is easy for a user to disclose information about someone else on social networking sites, or post photos they appear in.
- Discuss issues around privacy with the people you have friended and form some explicit agreements.
  - This is an issue that can only be handled through social relationships—and the norms that young people establish within their social group. It is also helpful for students to first think of how they would want their friends to treat their personal information and pictures.

- Suggested activity:
  - Some questions for students are these: How would you feel if someone came to a party, took an embarrassing picture of you, and posted it on Facebook and tagged you? How would you feel if you shared a personal problem you are having with someone whom you thought was a good friend and this person then posted this information on their profile? Have students work in teams to develop standards that they would want all of their friends to follow with respect to the information or photos their friends will share about them. Then in Golden Rule manner, restate this in terms of how they will respect their friends' privacy.

INSTRUCTIONAL OBJECTIVES

These instructional objectives should be adjusted based on how a teacher or school decides to handle the issue of underage users.

- (Grades 4–12) Students will describe the ways that social networking is allowing them to creatively demonstrate their personal identity and maintain connections with friends. Students will identify the risks that may be associated with these activities.
- (Grades 4–12) Students will describe how the terms of use of social networking sites prohibit actions that could cause harm to others or the site and how to file an abuse report.
- (Grades 4–12) Students will describe the privacy features that are provided on social networking sites, and explain how these features give them control over who can access their personal information or send messages. Students will express personal standards to safely guide their use of these features.
- (Grades 4–12) Students will describe how what they post on their profile may be used by others to form an impression of them and how this impression can impact their reputation, personal relationships, and opportunities. Students will express personal standards regarding what they will post on a social networking profile and in comments on the profiles of others. Students will recognize that although they may exercise control in sending information in electronic format to a select group of people, it is quite easy for anyone in that group to share this material further.

- (Grades 4–12) Students will explain how the process of "friending" allows others to form relationships with them, including people whom they know as well as people whom they might not know face-to-face, and that establishing a friendship link with an unknown or unsafe person could potentially result in risk or harm. Students will express personal standards for establishing friendship connections with people who are trustworthy and distinguishing between different types of friends.
- (Grades 4–12) Students will describe how the material they post or actions they engage in may place their friends or others at risk, could invade their privacy, or could cause other harm.

Embrace Civility
Prevent Hurtful Digital Communications

C*yberbullying* is the use of digital communication technologies to intentionally engage in repeated or widely disseminated acts of cruelty toward another that results in emotional harm.[1] The term *digital aggression* would be a better description of what is happening. These situations range from conflict to more traditional bullying, which involves an imbalance in power. A term that many teens apply to these situations is simply *drama*.[2]

Digital aggression can range from minor incidents to devastating harm. These incidents can happen 24/7 and be very public. Most often, it appears these situations involve both digital aggression and in-person disputes.

As digital aggression is clearly within the arena of health and wellness, in-depth instruction on these issues is likely best handled by health teachers or counselors, with additional insight provided by a law officer.

TYPES OF INCIDENTS

The following are different kinds of incidents that can be considered digital aggression:

---

[1] The author's other book, *Cyberbullying and Cyberthreats: Responding to the Challenge of Online Social Aggression, Threats, and Distress* (2007, Research Press) provides extensive insight into these concerns. Another excellent resource is Patchin, J. W., & Hinduja, S. (Eds.). (2011). *Cyberbullying prevention and response: Expert perspectives*. New York, NY: Routledge.

[2] Boyd, D. (2010, November 15). "Bullying" has little resonance with teenagers. *DML Central*. Retrieved June 22, 2011, from http://dmlcentral.net/blog/danah-boyd/bullying-has-little-resonance-teenagers

- *Flaming.* Online "fights" using digital messages with angry and vulgar language. These situations generally involve aggressors with equivalent strength.
- *Harassment.* Repeatedly sending offensive and insulting messages. This is the online equivalent to direct bullying.
- *Denigration.* Sending or posting cruel gossip or rumors about a person to damage his or her reputation or friendships. This is the online equivalent to indirect bullying, but frequently with wider dissemination.
- *Exclusion.* Intentionally excluding someone from an online group. For example, a group of people who all "unfriend" someone at one time. The online equivalent to relational aggression, "You are not our friend."
- *Impersonation.* Impersonating someone to make that person look bad, get that person in trouble or danger, or damage that person's reputation or friendships. This is a new form of aggression made possible by the ability to create a fake profile.
- *Outing.* Sharing someone's secrets or embarrassing information or photos online. This form of aggression is made possible because targets may put damaging information or photos in digital format that others can then send on to embarrass them.
- *Trickery.* Tricking someone into revealing secrets or embarrassing information, which is shared; deceiving someone online to humiliate or cause harm. This new form of aggression is made possible because it is easier to deceive someone online and then obtain damaging information that can be shared.
- *Cyberstalking.* Engaging in online activities that make a person afraid for her or her safety; using technology for control in an abusive dating relationship. Includes many of the preceding forms of aggression. This form of cyberbullying frequently occurs in the context of a failed personal relationship. Actions this egregious can be considered criminal.

How big of a problem is cyberbullying? The researchers at the Cyberbullying Research Center recently did an analysis of forty-two academic published studies on cyberbullying.[3] The reported incident rates ranged from 5.5 percent to 71 percent. It all depends on how questions were asked and how the studies were designed. A better estimate is that around 20 percent of young people have experienced some form of cyberbullying. However, there is a range of harmfulness. In the EU Kids Online survey, 55 percent of those who received harmful messages were very or fairly

---

[3] Patchin & Hinduja, supra.

upset, while 45 percent only a bit upset or not upset at all.[4] Furthermore, 62 percent got over it right away, while 8 percent were upset a few weeks or longer.

Do not make statements that many young people are cyberbullying. This expression of an inaccurate negative norm just provides support for the perception that if you are angry, it is okay to send a hurtful message because everyone else is. Focus on the accurate positive norm. Not only is everyone not engaging in hurtful behavior; the majority of students do not like to see this occur and will think badly of the people who engage in such hurtful behavior. And because evidence of this hurtful behavior is often publicly available online, this has an even greater chance of damaging your reputation and friendships.

It appears that girls are slightly more likely to be victimized, and boys slightly more likely to report offending.[5] Involvement in cyberbullying either as a target or aggressor is correlated with lower self-esteem and suicide ideation and attempts, as well as school problems and delinquent behaviors such as aggression, rule breaking, and carrying a weapon.[6] These are reported correlations and should not be perceived as causation. Underlying issues related to youth risk behavior and ineffective social skills are likely causing all of these challenges.

The vast majority of targets are cyberbullied by someone they know.[7] Furthermore, the existence of an in-person relationship increases the emotional distress. These situations are often far more complicated than one student attacking another. The EU Kids Online study revealed that 19 percent of youth reported that someone had acted in a hurtful or nasty way toward them in the past twelve months—13 percent in person, 6 percent on the Internet, and 3 percent on cell phones.[8] But of those targeted online, 10 percent had bullied others in person, and 41 percent had bullied others online. Researchers at the Cyberbullying Research Center in the United States identified that "revenge" for other harm is cited most frequently as the reason for engaging in cyberbullying.[9]

An important study by Drs. Hay and Meldrum revealed that both bullying and cyberbullying are correlated with suicide ideation in some youth.[10] However, the young people who demonstrated greater resiliency

---

[4] Livingstone et al., supra.

[5] Hinduja & Patchin, supra.

[6] Ybarra, M. L., Diener-West, M., & Leaf, P. J. (2007). Examining the overlap in Internet harassment and school bullying: Implications for school intervention. *Journal of Adolescent Health, 41*, S42–S50.

[7] Patchin & Hinduja, supra.

[8] Livingstone et al., supra.

[9] Patchin & Hinduja, supra.

[10] Hay & Meldrum, supra.

and less distress in response to bullying or cyberbullying also demonstrated a high level of individual self-control. That is, they had the ability to avoid responding impulsively, to moderate their emotional reaction to the situation, and to moderate their response. This is the most important issue that we need to address. If we can increase the ability of young people to respond to these situations in an effective manner and encourage a "cooling off" period before responding—avoid the impulse—this will hopefully reduce the degree to which conflict situations grow into really hurtful situations.

As was discussed in Chapter 3, it is imperative that schools avoid the use of curriculum or presenters who strive to reduce cyberbullying by focusing on the message, "Don't cyberbully or you could cause someone to suicide." This messaging is potentially very dangerous.

POLICY ISSUES AND DISCIPLINARY RESPONSES

The majority of digital aggression incidents are a continuation of—or in retaliation for—on-campus altercations.[11] Because these incidents are so closely related to on-campus altercations, they can negatively impact school climate and lead to a hostile environment or violence at school. Comprehensive bullying- and cyberbullying-prevention and -intervention initiatives are necessary.[12]

Frequently, there is confusion regarding whether school officials have the authority to formally respond to off-campus student speech.[13] There is strong legal precedence to conclude that regardless of where student hurtful speech has occurred, if that speech has, or reasonably could, cause a substantial disruption at school, school officials have the authority to respond. This includes situations that have or could result in violent altercations between students, significantly interfere with the ability of student to receive an education or participate in school activities, or create a significant interference in the delivery of instruction.

It is best that school district policies specifically state that school officials can and will respond to off-campus speech that meets this legal standard. Instructionally, the fact that school officials can intervene is an important point to communicate to students.

---

[11] Patchin & Hinduja, supra.

[12] These are discussed in Chapter 4.

[13] Willard, N. (2011). Cyberbullying and the law. In J. W. Patchin and S. Hinduja (Eds.), *Cyberbullying prevention and response: Expert perspectives* (pp. 36–56). New York, NY: Routledge.

BUILDING TEEN CAPACITY FOR PREVENTION AND RESPONSE

Research on cyberbullying and digital aggression has indicated that young people frequently do not report online incidents to adults either because they have already taken care of the situation or because they think they should be able to take care of these situations.[14]

This is developmentally appropriate. Teens need to be able to resolve the vast majority of personal altercation situations they get into by themselves. When they report to an adult, they may lose face with their peers and this can lead to greater problems. They will not tell adults, simply because we tell them to tell adults. They will only tell adults if adults are viewed as being helpful and effective in resolving the problem.

USING SOCIAL INFLUENCE FOR PREVENTION

As described in the Chapter 1, Drs. Craig and Perkins have had excellent success in reducing bullying behavior by demonstrating to the students that the social norms in their school do not support actions by others that are hurtful.[15] The survey and other responses from your school community will reveal that the vast majority of the students do not like this kind of negative drama. Furthermore, when these actions take place in a digital environment, many people will know who is engaging in behavior of which the vast majority of students do not approve.

Because They Are Different

Address the social climate that appears to support putting people down or treating them badly because they are different.[16] Disparaging others because they are different may appear to some to be the acceptable norm. There is also a social pecking order in schools where stronger students sometimes pick on students identified as weaker or different. It is imperative that we focus on positive social norms to change the perception that picking on someone who is different is acceptable behavior. This, in fact, may be the major social rights issue for this young generation—the positive social benefit of embracing our differences.

---

[14] Wolak et al. (2006), supra; Juvonen & Gross, supra.

[15] Craig & Perkins, supra.

[16] Rodkin, P. C. (2011, March 10). *Bullying and children's peer relationships.* Paper presented at the White House Conference on Bullying Prevention. Retrieved June 22, 2011, from http://www.stopbullying.gov/references/white_house_conference/index.html

They Probably Deserved It

Students may rationalize digital aggression as a response to something that the person who is targeted has done to them or someone else.[17] It does appear that sometimes digital aggression has been stimulated in response to behavior on the part of the person who is being targeted. These kinds of situations raise attention to the need to help young people find better ways of resolving conflict, without resorting to attacking the person who is causing them to feel upset.

Attention-Getting "Drama"

Another issue appears to be relevant in the issue of preventing cyberbullying is the issue of attention-getting.[18] We must create environments where young people don't get validated for negative attention and where they don't see relationship drama as part of normal life.

Relationship Issues

Especially in high school, issues related to relationships are often involved. This can include conflict between people who have been in a relationship or drama related to relationships, that is, fights over who can be in a relationship with whom. Often, it appears that students who are not handling relationships or sexuality issues in a healthy manner end up being targeted.

PREVENTION

Don't Provide the Ammunition

Students should know to avoid doing something online that provides "ammunition" for others. Warn students against posting or privately sending material others can use against them, accidentally offending others by not being careful how they communicate, and hanging around places where they are being treated badly. Also, if they have inadvertently or in a rash moment offended someone, immediately acknowledging this and offering an apology can often stop the situation from escalating.

Avoid Harmful Acts

Reinforce the use of positive social norms to enhance the inclination of students to effectively avoid engaging in harmful behavior. There

---

[17] Patchin & Hinduja, supra; Livingstone et al., supra.

[18] Rodkin, supra; Boyd, supra.

are key influences that can be used to work against engaging in hurtful behavior.

- The fact that everyone can see their postings and evidence of their hurtful behavior is recorded in digital format so that they can be held accountable for their actions
- The fact that a majority of students do not approve of this kind of hurtful behavior, as demonstrated by the survey and student discussions
- Reflecting on how they would feel if someone did something like this to them
- Thinking about what respected adults would think about them
- The reality that digital aggression, if it crosses the line, can lead to school discipline or could even be considered a criminal act

EFFECTIVE SKILLS FOR RESPONSE

Help students figure out how to prevent, deescalate, and stop these situations when they do get started.

Responses of Targets

The most important step in an effective response if they are under attack is to not respond when still angry and emotionally upset. If they wait to calm down and consider their options, they will be much more effective. It is very helpful for them to take the time to talk with a trusted friend or adult before doing anything. The corollary to this is not retaliating. Demonstrating that the person engaging in hurtful actions has effectively gotten you angry only rewards the aggressor—and could make others think both parties are equally at fault.

Saving the evidence and figuring out who the person causing the harm is are two important initial response steps. Sometimes, however, it may be difficult to determine who the aggressor is.

Then, the young person must figure out how to respond. The possible responses are very dependent on the situation.

- Is this a situation where it is unlikely that a response by the target will be effective? If so, seeking the assistance of a trusted peer or adult to step in will be the best choice.
- Has the student who is being targeted intentionally or inadvertently done something hurtful to the person who is now engaging in retaliation or to a friend of this person? If so, an apology may be in order.

- Is this a situation that is escalating online that is best resolved in person? If so, the target might initiate an in-person effort to resolve the situation.
- Is this just a heated situation that both students simply need to walk away from and not associate with each other for a while either in person or by using digital technologies? If so, suggesting a mutual "truce" and period of no contact may be an appropriate path. A mutual friend may be able to help negotiate a truce.
- Does the situation involve a digital fight between two people who have been in a close relationship that is now breaking up? In this situation, acknowledging the pain and suggesting a cooling off time might be appropriate.

Engage students in developing a list of the kinds of situations they have witnessed (not using names). Have them practice language they could use to respond digitally. They might keep the list of suggested written responses as a script for the next time one of these situations starts.

The other objective is to make it easier for young people who are targeted to report these incidents to adults. This can be done in a variety of ways:

- Communicate trust that they will be able to handle many of these situations on their own, but that sometimes it is simply necessary to obtain assistance from someone who has greater authority over the person who is causing harm
- Reframe that asking an adult for help is not a sign of weakness, but a sign that they will simply not put up with being harmed; adults sometimes also have to ask for help from someone with higher authority, like a human relations department, an attorney, or even the police
- Indicate that one way in which adults can help is by providing "invisible assistance" so that the student is perceived as responding on his or her own

Responding as the Aggressor

Discuss how to respond if they are the ones who have posted hurtful material or sent hurtful messages and either have been asked to stop or realize that what they have done was inappropriate. Too often, it is our perspective that people who engage in aggressive behavior are "the evil ones" who must be punished. Help young people learn the skills necessary to effectively proceed if they have done something that they now recognize was wrong. It would be helpful to engage students in brainstorming of the kinds of things that those who have engaged in harm can do to remedy the situation—and their reputation. Reinforce the positive social norm that someone who has caused harm, who then seeks to remedy the harm, is viewed by his or her peers in a favorable manner.

Responding as Helpful Allies

Encourage young people to provide leadership as helpful allies in stopping these incidents. As has been discussed, especially in situations of digital aggression, witnesses can become hurtful participants, passive observers, or helpful allies. Strategies to encourage positive peer intervention and a script for helpful allies to use in responding to hurtful situations were provided in Chapters 1 and 9. Students should be reminded that saying "stop" does not mean retaliating or doing something that could escalate the situation.

One particular strategy that can be recommended in situations involving digital aggression is the "Power of Three." Sometimes young people are afraid to intervene in situations where someone is engaging in hurtful conduct because they fear they will also come under attack. An advantage of digital communications is the ability to "invisibly" coordinate a positive intervention. If one student sees something posted online that is hurtful, that student can quickly contact several friends and plan a coordinated response. It is often better for people to contact the one engaging in harmful conduct privately, rather than a public challenge. But sometimes a public challenge is necessary. Planning an arranged intervention where three or more people, within a very short period of time, say "stop" can quickly turn the tide and stop the harm from escalating.

STOPPING FLAME WARS—AND REPORTING

Flame wars are online fights that start small and build, frequently getting angrier and angrier and involving many more students. All students have important responsibilities in stopping flame wars. Those involved in an incident that appears to be growing need to simply back off or be proactive and apologize. Those who are witnesses might be able to step in and stop the fight if it is its early stages. Students must also know the importance of reporting flame wars involving students to school officials, because frequently these flame wars lead to violence.

THREATS

Young people who are under high distress and potentially could engage in an act of violence against themselves or others are quite likely posting material online that provides evidence of these concerns. The FBI calls this *leakage*—when a student intentionally or unintentionally reveals clues to feelings, thoughts, fantasies, attitudes, or intentions that may signal an impending violent act against self or others.[19] Threatening or distressing material is far more likely to be witnessed by other young people, therefore encouraging students to report is critically important.

Students should be advised to be alert to the postings of others that express feelings of hopelessness, feeling trapped, seeing no reason for living, or a desire for revenge.[20] These might be writings, images, or photos. Postings about death or suicide are a special concern. Additional concerns would be any evidence that they are seeking information online about how to commit suicide or violence or are participating in any online communities that appear to encourage suicide or violence.

Advise students to always report material that appears to be threatening to a responsible adult, even if they are not sure it is real. Because if it is real, someone could get hurt. They should be sure to provide the exact online location of any posted materials. Because this material may be on a privacy protected profile, the witness may need to assist adults in accessing the material. The material can also be printed and provided to an adult.

Young people make threats all of the time, but they are generally not real threats. They may say something threatening as a joke or if angry. When these comments are said, others can view the entirety of the situation to determine if the threat is real or not. When threatening material is posted online, it is harder to tell whether or not the threat is real. Adults must respond as if these postings are real—which can lead to arrest, expulsion, and similar very bad consequences.

Advise students of the importance of not posting or sending any material that others, especially adults, might perceive to be a threat. Threatening to harm someone or destroy their property is a crime. It is not very smart to post material that provides evidence of the commission of, or intent to commit, a crime.

INSTRUCTIONAL ACTIVITIES

Instruction in this area should largely be focused on analysis of stories—both completed stories and setup stories. Student discussion of these stories should focus on understanding motivations and generating options for action that include scripts of what they might say. Students should

---

[19] O'Toole, M. E. (2000). *The school shooter: A threat assessment perspective.* Federal Bureau of Investigation. Retrieved June 22, 2011, from www.fbi.gov/stats-services/publications/school-shooter

[20] Suicide Prevention Resource Center. (2010, January 5). *Customized information: Teens.* Retrieved June 22, 2011, from http://www.sprc.org/featured_resources/customized/teens.asp

always be encouraged to think of several possible action options, because the first one might not be effective. A necessary option to include if the situation is serious or unresolved is to talk with a trusted adult.

An analysis of the actual survey data can also be helpful. Engage students in an analysis of the data related to responses and effectiveness. Also, analyze the data regarding values and actions related to digital aggression. Turn this data into effective messaging.

INSTRUCTIONAL OBJECTIVES

- (Grades 4–12) Students will recognize that the majority of students do not like it when people are hurtful using digital technologies, that many students are willing to take steps to stop this kind of harm, and that other students and adults highly respect those who reach out to help others.

- (Grades 4–12) Students will describe reasons to avoid engaging in hurtful digital behavior, including the fact that they would not like it if someone did this to them, that this material is available in digital format that thus can damage their reputation among their peers who do not like to see this occur, that their parents would disapprove of this kind of behavior, and that evidence may also lead to other consequences.

- (Grades 4–12) Students will recognize how their online postings or communications might place them at risk and will develop personal standards so that what they post cannot be used to cause harm to them.

- (Grades 4–12) Students will explain how a cycle of aggression that involves hurtful digital acts that lead to retaliation can grow to a point where all parties are being harmed, and will describe strategies that can be used to effectively stop the expansion of such hurtful digital behavior.

- (Grades 4–12) Students will describe effective strategies they can use if someone engages in online hurtful digital behavior that targets them, including taking the time to calm down and consider possible actions, not engaging in retaliation, and saving the evidence and identify the aggressor. Steps they can take to independently resolve the problem include leaving the site, ignoring or blocking the person, contacting the person and trying to resolve the conflict, calmly and strongly telling the person to stop, asking a mutual friend to help resolve the conflict, and filing an abuse report with the site or service.

- (Grades 4–12) Students will describe ways in which adults can help stop online hurtful digital behavior, including providing "invisible guidance" to help them respond to the situation, contacting this person's parents, obtaining assistance from the school, and contacting an attorney or the police.

- (Grades 4–12) Students will recognize that the majority of their peers do not approve of hurtful digital behavior and think badly of people who engage in such behavior, and that retaliating online to someone who is being hurtful to them will not resolve the problem and could lead to their being blamed for the problem.

- (Grades 4–12) Students will develop personal standards to avoid engaging in online aggression. They will demonstrate skills in resolving a conflict situation that they have started, including removing hurtful material, publicly or privately apologizing, and advising others about the negative impact of engaging in hurtful digital behavior.

- (Grades 4–12) Students will recognize that as witnesses to hurtful digital behavior, they can play an exceptionally important role in preventing the continuation of the harm including providing emotional support to the person who is being harmed, trying to resolve the conflict, publicly or privately telling the person causing harm to stop, and filing an abuse report. They will recognize that it is important to report serious or unresolved concerns to a responsible adult.

- (Grades 4–12) Students will recognize the seriousness of material posted online that appears to threaten an act of violence against self or others. Students will know to avoid posting or sending material that others could view as threatening and the importance of promptly and effectively reporting such material to a responsible adult.

Cyberdate Safely

Avoid Exploitation and Abusive Relationships

Teens, technology, and sex—the combination of these three issues is guaranteed to make many adults very nervous. The issues addressed in this chapter are also best addressed in-depth by health teachers and counselors, with additional insight provided by law enforcement officers.

Different communities will have different perceptions on what age is best to introduce topics related to digital activities related to sexuality, exploitation, and personal relationships. The "Think Before You Post" and "Connect Safely" messaging addresses issues that relate to the sexual and relationship concerns more generally. However, it should be noted that many middle schools are reporting problems with students engaging in sexting. A frequent age for predators to target is younger teens. Likely, these discussions should be initiated in fifth grade in the context of sex-education instruction. By no later than eighth grade, all of these issues should be more fully addressed. This is essential preparation for the expanded relationship challenges students will face as they enter high school.

HELPFUL ONLINE ACTIVITIES

Do not lose focus on the fact that there are helpful online activities related to sexuality and relationships. Students can

- find sexual health information on high quality websites;
- receive support, including relationship support, through professional support sites; and
- further healthy personal relationships.

The teenage years are when young people will start exploring issues related to personal and sexual relationships. We must expect that they will using digital technologies within the context of these relationships.

SEXUAL PREDATORS: CORRECT THE MYTHS

As discussed in Chapter 3, there are significant concerns about inaccurate information related to the issue of online sexual predation. The following, from the website of the Crimes Against Children Research Center (CACRC), outlines the issue quite clearly:

> The publicity about online "predators" who prey on naive children using trickery and violence is largely inaccurate. Internet sex crimes involving adults and juveniles more often fit a model of statutory rape—adult offenders who meet, develop relationships with, and openly seduce underage teenagers—than a model of forcible sexual assault or pedophilic child molesting. This is a serious problem, but one that requires different approaches from current prevention messages emphasizing parental control and the dangers of divulging personal information. Developmentally appropriate prevention strategies that target youth directly and focus on healthy sexual development and avoiding victimization are needed. These should provide younger adolescents with awareness and avoidance skills, while educating older youth about the pitfalls of relationships with adults and their criminal nature. Particular attention should be paid to higher risk youth, including those with histories of sexual abuse, sexual orientation concerns, and patterns of off- and online risk taking.[1]

Based on the research findings, the CACRC suggests the following approach to education:

> This is a serious problem, but one that requires different approaches from current prevention messages emphasizing parental control and the dangers of divulging personal information. Developmentally appropriate prevention strategies that target youth directly and focus on healthy sexual development and

---

[1] Crimes Against Children Research Center. (n.d.). Internet. Retrieved June 22, 2011, from http://www.unh.edu/ccrc/internet-crimes/. All of the material in this section is grounded in the research of the CACRC. This research can be found under the "Papers" link on this webpage. See especially Wolak, J., Finkelhor, D., Mitchell, K., & Ybarra, M. (2008). Online "predators" and their victims: Myths, realities and implications for prevention and treatment. *American Psychologist, 63*, 111–128. Retrieved June 22, 2011, from http://www.unh.edu/ccrc/internet-crimes/papers.html

avoiding victimization are needed. These should provide younger adolescents with awareness and avoidance skills, while educating older youth about the pitfalls of relationships with adults and their criminal nature. Particular attention should be paid to higher risk youth, including those with histories of sexual abuse, sexual orientation concerns, and patterns of off- and online risk taking.

- Avoid descriptions of the problem that characterize victims as young children or emphasize violence and deception.
- Be clear about why sex with underage adolescents is wrong.
- Focus prevention efforts more on adolescents, less on parents, and frankly on concerns relevant to adolescents, including autonomy, romance and sex.
- Focus prevention more on interactive aspects of Internet use and less on posting personal information.
- Educate youth about criminal behavior and child pornography.
- Develop targeted prevention approaches for the most at-risk youth populations.
- Assess for patterns of risky online behavior.[2]

Unfortunately, much focus related to online sexual predators has been on dangerous adult strangers. Adult family members and acquaintance sexual abusers, who are by far the majority of the sex offenders, could also use communication technologies for grooming and control. The following are the manipulation strategies used most often by sexual predators:[3]

- *Being overly friendly.* What do vulnerable teens crave? Positive attention. What do predators provide? Positive attention—and lots of it. "Wow, you are hot." "Hey, you are really cool." "You are so sexy." "I am so happy I met you."
- *Seeming overly eager.* Predators are overly eager to form a relationship. "You are my new 'best friend.'" "You can trust me and talk about anything." "I will always be there for you."
- *Rewarding with victim for taking one step at a time.* Predators will reward steps that come closer and closer to their objective. "Wow, you are so sexy, send me an even sexier pix." "Wow, this is really hot. Can you really show me your stuff?"

---

[2] Crimes Against Children Research Center, supra.

[3] O'Connell, R. (2003) *A typology of child cybersexpolitation and online grooming practices.* Cyberspace Research Unit, University of Lanchester, UK. Retrieved June 22, 2011, from http://www.jisc.ac.uk/uploaded_documents/lis_PaperJPrice.pdf

- *Threatening a loss.* Predators may threaten a loss to encourage other actions. "If you really loved me, you would send me a nude pix." "If you won't have sex with me, I will send your nude pix to others."

It is also important to recognize that some teens are using are using technologies to seek sexual "hookups"—which, depending on the age and initial inclinations of the parties, could constitute sexual exploitation. Warn older high school students about this. This is a very significant concern after they turn eighteen. If they attempt to solicit sex with a minor online, especially if they ask for or send a nude photo, they face arrest and registration as a sex offender—even if under the "safe haven" provisions of your state's statutory rape laws, they could legally have sex with this minor.

Some of the criminal laws around these activities are behind the times when it comes to teen sexual activity online—some of which is exploitive and some of which is simply teen sexual activity online.[4] However, the "realities" of the criminal issues need to be discussed, especially when students are approaching eighteen, preferably by a law enforcement officer.

Sometimes teens also appear to be essentially "trafficking themselves" through their social networking profile. They may advertise sexual services on other sites. Or they may be acting under the control of a pimp. This a difficult issue to address through instruction. But teachers, counselors, and school resource officers must be attentive to this possible activity. If a student is engaging in this kind of activity, it is likely that some other students are aware of this, thus reinforcing the importance of being a helpful ally if they know someone who is engaging in online sexual risk behavior and report this to a responsible adult.

FANTASY LOVE

Fantasy love is cyberdating that becomes a fantasy. If a personal relationship is pursued primarily through digital communications, without the opportunity to interact in person, one or both of the parties can develop unrealistic understandings and expectations. The partners can get into a pattern of expressing feelings of love and appreciation—simply because it feels so nice to be receiving such loving messages.

Inevitably, reality will strike. At this point, one or both partners may feel betrayed, which can lead to vicious breakups. Unfortunately, in the context of these relationships, sexual photos or other material may have

---

[4] Willard, N. (2011). *Sexting and youth: Achieving a rational approach.* Center for Safe and Responsible Internet Use. Retrieved June 22, 2011, from http://www.csriu.org/documents/sextingandyouth.pdf

been shared. When the relationships break up, these photos or material become ammunition to cause harm, and the situation switches to digital aggression.

Help teens understand the dynamics of these online relationships so they will recognize the signs that they have gotten into a relationship that is a fantasy, avoid unrealistic expectations, and end relationships with understanding and kindness. Teens will understandably be angry and disappointed, and maybe a bit ashamed or embarrassed, but if they engage in attack, this will simply increase the harm to both. Simply walking away is preferable. Friends can be helpful in pointing out the signs of a fantasy love and suggesting positive ways to walk away.

DIGITAL DATING ABUSE

Abusive partners use technologies, most frequently cell phones, for manipulation and control.[5] Common abusive behaviors include

- excessive texting, including through the night, to find out where the person is and who is with the person;
- sexual harassment and sexual demands;
- demands for nude photos and then use of those photos for blackmail;
- demanding passwords for e-mail and social networking accounts; and
- placing demands on with whom their partner can establish a friendship link or communicate.

When addressing abusive relationships, it is necessary to address use of technologies for abuse and control.[6] Engage students in conversations about positive strategies to use digital technologies to enhance their personal relationships and how they can effectively handle situations if their partner's use of technologies has become abusive or controlling.

One of the challenges in these situations is that the focus is often solely on the abused partner and supporting this person to leave an abusive situation. Focus also on the emotional concerns of those partners who are engaging in this abusive behavior—because abusers are not going to

---

[5] MTV & Associated Press. (2009). *A thin line: 2009 AP-MTV digital abuse survey*. Retrieved June 22, 2011, from http://www.athinline.org/MTV-AP_Digital_Abuse_Study_Executive_Summary.pdf; Claiborne, L. (2007). *Love is not abuse. Technology and TeenDating Abuse Survey*. Retrieved June 22, 2011, from http://www.loveisnotabuse.com/statistics.htm

[6] The A Thin Line (http://www.athinline.org/) and That's Not Cool (http://www.thatsnotcool.org) websites are excellent resources.

stop until their own anxiety and other concerns are effectively addressed. Focus on how teens can engage in healthy relationships, recognize when their own behavior is causing concerns, and change this behavior.

SEXTING

Sexting is a term that has been applied to a range of digital sexual-related activity.[7] Most frequently, this is applied to the act of creating and disseminating revealing photos. It is helpful to clarify to students that the concerns are associated with photos that reveal the parts of their body that would normally be covered by a bathing suit. Sometimes the term *sexting* has also been used to refer to sending sexually explicit text messages. As noted in Chapter 3, inaccurate information is frequently disseminated about the percentage of young people engaging in sexting. A very small minority of young people appear to be engaging in this kind of activity. The teens who engage in these activities likely[8]

- want desperately to belong and fit in and find someone with whom they can form a close personal relationship;
- are impulsive, fail to recognize or consider the consequences of their behavior, and fail to use appropriate problem-solving strategies; and
- are using technologies that allow for the permanent digital recording and wide distribution of evidence of their mistakes in judgment.

There appear to be different kinds of sexting situations. Recognize that these are points within a range, not definitive classifications.[9]

- *Developmentally normative.* Private possession or mutually consenting situations where no one intended to hurt anyone and photos were supposed to remain private, but a mistake might have resulted in distribution.
- *Elements of harassment or ill intent.* Distribution outside of a consensual relationship, pressure to create and provide the photo.
- *Sexual solicitation.* The teen depicted appears to be soliciting sexual activity, which could range from attention-getting to sexual trafficking.

---

[7] Wolak, J., & Finklehor, D. (2011). Sexting: A typology. Crimes Against Children Research Center. Retrieved June 22, 2011, from http://www.unh.edu/ccrc/pdf/CV231_Sexting%20Typology%20Bulletin_4-6-11_revised.pdf

[8] Willard (2010), supra.

[9] Willard (2010), supra. The CACRC researchers have divided these into two groups: aggregated and experimental. Wolak & Finklehor, supra.

- *Sexual exploitation.* Situations where teens or adults have engaged in significant exploitation of other teens, sometimes involving a wider age difference.

In some of these situations, teen's involvement in sexting should be considered an early warning sign that the teen might be headed down a path toward victim or abuser that could, in the future, present even greater concerns. Thus, any sexting incident should be viewed as a red flag and evaluated to determine the necessary restorative approach. A significant concern that was revealed in a recent survey, conducted by MTV and the Associated Press, is that 61 percent of teens reported being pressured to provide photos.[10] There appear to be a range of situations related to such pressure—from peer or partner pressure up to manipulative grooming by predatory teens or adults.

In some jurisdictions, law enforcement has considered the creation and distribution of these nude photos as a criminal act under laws against child pornography.[11] These laws were enacted to prevent exploitation of minors by adults. In every jurisdiction, these statutes need to be revised. Recently, more enlightened legislative/law enforcement has taken the position that the majority of these incidents should be handled in a restorative, educational manner.

There is a major concern about telling teens that creating these photos could be considered a criminal act. If a teen has created and sent a photo to someone who is now using that photo for blackmail, the teen could fear reporting because of the potential for prosecution. Thus, fear of reporting could lead to additional exploitation and significant emotional harm. Those who use or distribute these photos for harmful purposes should be considered for prosecution.

Correct the misperception that many teens are sexting, given that the overwhelming majority are not. Encourage the actual positive social norm. Strive to stop the initial behavior—asking for or creating and sending a photo—to ward off other harms. Disseminating a photo that has been provided under conditions of trust is an act that most teens will consider to be unacceptable. There should also be some form of criminal consequence in response to such distribution, but the approach must be restorative.

It is presumed that with local surveying, an overwhelming majority will indicate that providing a revealing photo to anyone is about the stupidest thing someone could do. This demonstration of a positive social norm can provide significant value in situations where a student is trying

---

[10] MTV & Associated Press, supra.

[11] These concerns are outlined in Willard (2010), supra.

to pressure another student into providing such a photo. Imagine the benefit in preventing sexting of having posters around the school that say,

> 98 percent of the students in XYZ high school say that if someone asked them for a revealing photo, their response would be: "No way. Never. Good bye." Why? Because they know that once someone has that photo, it could easily be distributed and their reputation would be trashed.

Inevitably, in most schools, someone is going to make a mistake, and a photo is going to make the rounds. More frequently, photos of girls are distributed than photos of boys. In these situations, the person depicted is likely to be the recipient of significant harassment. It would be helpful to generate understanding in these situations that sometimes people place trust in others that is mistaken and strive to reduce the resulting sexual harassment. Encourage students who are recognized leaders to provide leadership in stopping the to-be-expected harassment and reporting such harassment to school officials.

INSTRUCTIONAL ACTIVITIES

Instruction addressing these issues should be handled in a similar manner to instruction about issues related to digital aggression. This should include discussions of stories, as well as analyses of local data. Identifying strategies for prevention and response are important.

INSTRUCTIONAL OBJECTIVES

- (Grades 4–12) Students will recognize that young people may use digital technologies to develop personal relationships. In a manner appropriate to their age, students will describe how Internet resources and technologies can be used for healthy sexual and relationship purposes.
- (Grades 6–12) Students will recognize risks associated with forming close personal relationships that are developed through the use of digital communications and describe effective strategies to prevent themselves from getting into risky situations, detect whether they are at risk, and respond, including the potential of furthering a relationship online

(Continued)

(Continued)

that is not grounded in a realistic understanding of the other person; how unsafe people might use the Internet to engage in seduction for the purpose of leading to sexual involvement, common grooming techniques used by such individuals, and the emotional and health risks associated with such involvement; how abusive partners can use technologies to abuse and maintain control; and that asking for, creating, or disseminating a revealing photo could lead to significant damage to their reputation and potentially legal trouble.

- (Grades 4–12) Students will recognize the potential harm to their friends from risky sexual and relationship activities, demonstrate skills in communicating to a friend how such involvement could lead to harm, and recognize the need to report serious or unresolved situations to a responsible adult.

Index

CORWIN

A SAGE Company

The Corwin logo—a raven striding across an open book—represents the union of courage and learning. Corwin is committed to improving education for all learners by publishing books and other professional development resources for those serving the field of PreK–12 education. By providing practical, hands-on materials, Corwin continues to carry out the promise of its motto: **"Helping Educators Do Their Work Better."**